FREED FROM SAT

'Many want to ignore the whole realm of the demonic, but for those involved it is very real. Vince's story shows that although Satan wants to appear powerful he is not all-powerful. This will be an encouragement to many still struggling with the need for deliverance from involvement in the occult.'

Doug Harris
Director of Reachout Trust

'There are so many doorways to danger in the occult and too many people today are carelessly wandering through them, especially the young and vulnerable. This is why I truly welcome Vince McCann's story of his fall into darkness and his rise to the light and life of Christianity.'

Kevin Logan
Author and Anglican minister

Freed from Satan's Grasp

VINCE McCANN

KINGSWAY PUBLICATIONS
EASTBOURNE

Contents

Acknowledgements

I would like to thank the following people who helped support me throughout the writing of this book:

My wife Donna and children Nathaniel and Edward, who exercised great patience and allowed me the time I needed to complete this work.

Pastor Mike Haynes and everyone at my church fellowship for their encouragement and prayer.

Helen McGeoch for the time spent proof reading.

Special thanks to Sue Smith for her commitment to this work and for doing an excellent job in editing the final manuscript.

Dedication

I dedicate this book to the memory of my late father, William McCann. Greatly missed and never forgotten.

* * *

Because this testimony is of a very dramatic nature I have felt it right to include a brief statement and dedication to God.

I (Vincent McCann) declare before God that this story is true. The many individuals included in this account can be called upon at any time to bear witness to the truthfulness of this testimony. I have nothing to hide. Everything has been told as it happened.

God is my judge.

Note: Some of the names of the individuals mentioned in this story have been changed to protect their identities.

Foreword

Dabble in Christianity and you shouldn't be too surprised if you meet the Holy Spirit – the powerful presence of God who can transform your life with joy and peace.

Dabble in the occult – from astrology to Zen – and equally you should not be amazed to find yourself grappling with an unholy spirit who can make your life hell.

There are so many doorways to danger in the occult and too many people today are carelessly wandering through them, especially the young and vulnerable.

This is why I truly welcome Vince McCann's story of his fall into the darkness of the occult and his rise to the light and life of Christianity. I had the privilege of meeting Vince in a television studio, as we both tried to persuade a vicar-turned-witch to turn again and come back to an almighty, loving God whom he had obviously never really got to know.

Vince is a level-headed, intelligent and caring man who is deeply concerned at the harm that the occult is causing in British society. I applaud his courage and integrity in telling his story.

I pray that it will help Christians to know more fully the

battle they fight, and also that it will be used to keep many from going through those occult and dangerous doorways.

Kevin Logan
Anglican vicar and author of
Paganism and the Occult,
Close Encounters with the New Age and
Satanism and the Occult

1
Puppet on a String

'Hurry up!' hissed Jane, between pursed lips, her white, elfin face contorted with rage. She glanced swiftly around to ensure that no passers-by in the small suburban street had heard her. Obediently, fearfully, I quickened my step, trudging behind her diminutive figure in a trance-like state, weary from lack of sleep, lack of food and the mental torment I was suffering.

I dared not argue. In fact, I no longer had the strength nor the will to argue, even if I had wanted to. All my resistance had long gone. Under her control, I was like a puppet on a string as I obeyed her commands, plodding along the deserted street, emotionally and mentally beaten as low as anyone could go. I had lost so much weight that for all the world I looked like a hopeless heroin addict. But I had never taken hard drugs; the power that held me was stronger than any drug.

I hadn't had a bath for ages – there was never the opportunity for such a luxury. Even if there had been, I doubt whether I would have bothered. I had lost all dignity and self-respect, and was rapidly losing what was left of my sanity. I knew that death was the only way out of the agony I was in. But even that seemed to escape me, at least for the moment. It was as though something in Jane's plan had to happen to me before I was allowed to take this step.

As we stopped outside the small, white bungalow where her parents lived, Jane seemed momentarily distracted, as though she was trying to work something out in her mind. She frowned down at the dirty pavement, her jet black hair swinging over her face like a curtain. I used the brief break to reflect upon what had become of my life. I longed to see my father, mother and brother again. A faint flicker of emotion burned inside me, temporarily dispelling the familiar hard feeling that I was now so accustomed to. My heart ached to be in their company once more. But as quickly as I thought about seeing them again, I put the idea out of my mind. They were in danger. Jane had told me that they would be harmed if I ever returned to stay with them. I knew this was no idle threat as I had witnessed the things she was capable of doing. The familiar hard feeling took over once more. It seemed as if I was being programmed like a robot to be incapable of any real human warmth and emotion.

Jane was still distracted, a rare thing as she usually watched my every move. Maybe she assumed that I had reached the stage where she could take her eyes off me now and then. Maybe she was just becoming careless. Whatever the reason, it gave me a fleeting moment of relief. Suddenly, something seemed to snap inside me. It was as if one of the puppet strings had slackened and in a split second, I took my chance and ran. I didn't know where I was running as I didn't have anywhere to go. A thought flashed through my mind: 'Make your way to the railway station and throw yourself under the next available train.' I had always had a vague belief that a God of some sort existed and that, since I wasn't such a bad person, I would probably be welcome in heaven when I died. Yet I quickly dismissed this thought. Now that I actually had an opportunity to take my life, I found that I couldn't go ahead with it after all. I was too scared. 'What if there *isn't* a heaven *or* a God after all?' I thought. So I continued to run, without hope and without direction. All I knew was that I had to get away from the hellish situation I was in and the pitiless puppeteer who had me in her grip.

After running about half way up the road with only the sound of my feet hitting the pavement of the quiet street and the muffled thumping of my frantic heartbeat, I heard Jane's voice roaring loudly and deeply, 'Vince! Vince! Come back *now*!' At first, I ignored the words and continued my escape, but the shouts persisted as she ran after me. 'It's hopeless,' I thought. 'Even if I did get away, where would I go?' The enthusiasm for escape that had originally empowered me began to drain away. I felt like a wind-up toy that begins with a burst of energy as it is wound up as far as it can go, but then eventually winds down to its inevitable halt. 'Vince!' Jane bellowed in a commanding voice once more. But now her voice was louder and angrier and she had gained on me. As she got closer, she ordered 'Stop!' in a voice that was powerful, authoritative, and seemed too deep for a young girl. This final command stopped me dead in my tracks and I became limp and listless again. She caught me up, her white face now red with anger and exertion, her eyes bulging and screamed, 'Where do you think you are going?'

'I have had enough,' I replied. 'I was going to kill myself. I want to go to heaven.'

She laughed scornfully and pointed at the ground. 'The only place you are going is down there! Now come on!' With these words, we made our way back to the bungalow. I knew that the torment was to continue. I shuddered with absolute dread and despair as I imagined what might be in store for me. After the things I had seen and experienced, it seemed as if anything could be possible.

As I trailed reluctantly to the front door of the innocent-looking bungalow, I wondered again how I had got to such a state. How did I, a young man from a poor, but stable family background, find myself in such an extreme predicament? If, earlier in my life, someone had told me of the incredible events which would lead up to this awful situation, I would have laughed in their face. Yet here I was, not so many years later, hopeless and desperate, hardly recognizable as the same person.

2
Early Days

I was born in Birkenhead, Wirral (just over the water from Liverpool) on August 16th 1969. We lived in a high-rise block of flats in a rough area of town called Beauford Square. Our block overlooked wasteland and was close to a very noisy railway track. My earliest memories were happy enough, however, because even though we were very poor, my parents always made us feel loved and wanted, though they themselves felt the pressure of our poverty. My younger brother, Kevin, and I played a lot together and, despite the odd argument, got on pretty well most of the time. I can remember cycling round and round the block on my three-wheeler tricycle, merrily ringing the bell to my heart's content. My bike was my prize possession, especially as we never had much in the way of material items.

Life was not all pleasant, though, particularly when it came to making friends with the other kids in the area. I was only about three years old when I learnt the hard lesson of how cruel children can be to each other. A group of boys used to play with their action men figures in a mud pit on a field over the road from our block. One day I joined them and, to my delight, they let me play with one of their figures.

Naturally, it wasn't long before I wanted a figure of my own and pestered my mother for one. Finally giving in to the constant pleas, she bought me a figure that *looked* like an action man but was not actually the real thing. It was a cheap imitation version and not as sophisticated as the other children's figures. Unlike the serious-looking, muscular action men that the other children had, mine had a smiling face, a skinny body and a squeezable head!

Not realizing that my action man wasn't of the same quality, I proudly rushed out to meet the other children and display my new toy to them. Their reaction was to erupt into raucous laughter, snatch my action man from me and squeeze its head, saying: 'That's not a proper action man!' They swung my figure all round the field and covered it in mud. I was devastated as I fled the scene followed by a hail of mocking jeers.

These sorts of experiences made me retreat into myself, expressing my insecurity through my play, as young children do. I was increasingly attracted to anything dark, strange and unusual. I have very early memories of drawing lots of pictures of gruesome monsters. My parents would look over my shoulder and ask me why I was drawing such pictures and try to encourage me to draw 'nice pictures' instead. But despite their concerns, my interest in dark things grew, albeit very slowly and imperceptibly. Even my toys took on a somewhat macabre theme. I became fascinated with toy skeletons and began to amass a collection of them in various styles and sizes.

When I was four years old, we moved from Beauford Square to Tollemache Road a few miles away. This was to be home for me for the rest of my childhood and most of my teenage years. Tollemache Road was situated on the outskirts of the notorious 'North End' area of Birkenhead. The area had a bad name throughout the rest of the Wirral and no one really wanted to live there. People who were in search of a council house would go to the housing office in town and repeat the mantra of: 'I don't want a house in the North End', knowing that these were the first houses they would be offered. My father was no exception and he too was offered a house in that area of town. After refusing this, he was offered a house a bit further away. As this new house was not exactly in the heart of the dreaded North End, my father reasoned that it was acceptable.

My brother and I had trouble fitting in with some of the other local kids and were often viewed as 'outsiders'. As a result, we frequently had to flee from a feared gang who called themselves 'The Wreck'. These were older boys who used to spend most of their time hanging round the local recreation field (hence the nickname – rec /wreck).

There were about eight boys in the Wreck gang and they often wore the same distinctive style of clothing; colourful, sporty, ski coats. This uniform was pretty useful for Kev and me, as we could usually see them coming a mile off and make a hasty get-away! But we couldn't rely on this warning device, and were sometimes caught by surprise.

One such evening was when we were in a state of high excitement because it had been snowing heavily for a few days. We were busily rolling a large snowball across the ground towards some fencing when suddenly we felt snowballs hitting us in the back. Thinking it might have been some friends, we looked round, ready to retaliate, but to our horror, we saw instead the Wreck gang walking purposefully towards us, with fierce expressions on their faces. Worse still, some of them were holding large blocks of ice. Cold and hard as the ice they held, the boys knocked us to the ground and began hurling the blocks at us. All we could do was crouch into a terrified ball and hope that the battering would soon be over. The beating proceeded in an almost business-like manner and we cowered as the painful ice thumped off our backs like some manic drumming. And then, as suddenly as it began, it was over. The silent menace departed and we were left with some nasty bruises, but counting ourselves fortunate that we were not more seriously injured.

Despite the hostilities, we did make one good friend, Mark, an older boy who lived a few doors down from us. We looked up to him as if he were a big brother and followed all his fads and interests. When we were out and about with him and he met friends his own age from school, he would urge us to say that we were his brothers, to save him the embarrassment of being seen to hang around with younger kids!

Early experiences of school were not good. Both my brother and I went to a school in Birkenhead called Cavendish. To my dismay, I quickly discovered that some of the Wreck gang also went to this school. I can still recall the cold, sinking feeling of dread in the pit of my stomach when I noticed the familiar face of one of the gang members grinning at me in a taunting manner. As a result, I was always looking over my shoulder and I soon learnt to become a fast runner!

I was not the most studious of students and often found myself drifting off during lessons, wishing I was somewhere else. Owing to my lack of concentration and general un-willingness to be in school, I often got into trouble for not completing my work and was pigeonholed into the 'non-academic' category.

In an attempt to get by, I made sure I sat next to one of the cleverer kids in the class, John Earl (who is still a good friend to this day). While the teacher wasn't looking, I used to copy reams and reams of his work into my book and proudly hand it in as my own. At the time, I didn't realize that I was really storing up trouble for myself later on in life. Rather than develop my own learning, I picked up a bad habit of copying other people's work throughout the rest of my years in school.

Because of my academic struggles and apparent inability to grasp basic schoolwork, my parents were forced to trans-fer me to a school for children with learning difficulties when I was nine years old. This was a traumatic time for me as I found myself in a strange environment with children I didn't know. To make matters worse, I soon discovered that some of the children at the school not only had difficulties with their schoolwork, but also had severe emotional problems.

One skinny little fair-haired boy with angelic features used to erupt into a fury at the slightest thing that bothered him. The contrast in his behaviour was memorable because it was so extreme. One moment he would be softly spoken, polite and cheerful, then, in an instant, he would transform into a red-faced rage, swearing, throwing tables and chairs around the classroom, and swinging punches at the nearest teacher (or anyone who got in his way).

Over time, however, I did make a couple of close friends. We were in a small group who spent a lot of our time running around the playground pretending to be car drivers. At break times, we were a familiar sight as we raced around the playground with arms stretched in front of us holding onto invisible steering wheels, making 'brumm, brumm' noises and screeching brake sounds. I wasn't particularly interested in cars, but in an attempt to fit in, I can remember forcing myself to race around the playground to gain the friendship of at least some people.

After spending about a year at this school, my work improved sufficiently to go back to Cavendish. It was very difficult to go back as I felt like a stranger. The school seemed to be full of mean kids who were from really rough areas of town. In the playground I felt as if everyone was glaring at me and nobody wanted to know me. I spent a lot of time wandering around alone and consequently became an easy target for bullies.

On top of all this, some members of the Wreck gang were *still* in the school, in the top year. Their attitude towards me was worse than ever. I hated school so much at this time and would plead with my mother not to send me. I faked a lot of illnesses in an attempt to stay away, and most of the time my efforts paid off, with the result that the education authorities became frequent visitors to our house, to find out why I was missing so much school.

Somehow, I managed to survive my time at Cavendish and I moved on to Park High School. In spite of a bit of a bumpy start, I soon settled in and even began to enjoy myself. Various factors made this possible. First, none of the Wreck gang were there, as they had all gone on to another school. Also, I felt as if I had the chance to start school afresh and was pleased to discover that I quickly made a small number of good friends. I still wasn't a very confident young person and it took me some time to feel as if I was accepted.

As time went on, I, like most teenage boys, began to notice girls in a whole new light! Even girls I had known for some time as friends suddenly began to take on a new attractiveness. But because of shyness, I rarely made the effort to say anything meaningful to the girls I was really attracted to. It seemed that the more I was drawn to a particular girl, the more terrified I was of her! Needless to say, I didn't have a lot of luck with this approach.

Though I didn't make much headway with girls at this time, I did seem to be achieving a new status with my male peers. Looking back, I now understand that one of the reasons why people liked having me around in school was because I laughed at their humour and antics. I came to realize that people enjoyed being in the company of those who make them feel witty and humorous. This insight served me well, especially in the last year of school, as our class was virtually run by two bullies, who were both called John. If you got on the wrong side of them, they made your life a living hell, but if they liked you, school was a whole lot sweeter. They seemed to have such a control on the whole class that they were capable of starting a miniature revolution at a moment's notice. On more than one occasion, the two Johns decided that the whole class would refuse to go into a particular lesson and bunk off. Those who opposed them were severely dealt with through physical or verbal intimidation.

One boy in the class, Jimmy, made the mistake of going to the teacher to inform them of some wrong-doing that the two Johns had been involved in. He seemed blissfully unaware of the unwritten school rule that 'no matter what happens to you, you should never go and tell a teacher on a classmate'. To do so was like breaking some sort of holy code and those who dared break it were smeared with the belittling label of 'grass'. Jim had broken this code, and as a result his life became a misery. It seemed that on a daily basis he was intimidated and bullied.

I can remember on one occasion, while the teacher was out of the classroom, the two Johns locked Jimmy in a large metal cabinet and then proceeded to kick, punch and drop the cabinet around the room. They only opened it up at various intervals to spit at him, after which they continued to beat it like a drum. When he was eventually released from his box of torment, he emerged shaken and covered from head to toe in spit. Nobody dared intervene or tell the teacher what had happened, as we all secretly feared similar things happening to us.

In an attempt to be in with the main crowd, I ended up getting into a lot of mischief and consequently often got hit with a cane as punishment. There was one teacher, Mr Kent, who used to take those of us who had been caught in some sort of misbehaviour, and make us stand together in a line, against a wall, as though we were waiting for the firing squad. He paced up and down in front of us like a sergeant inspecting his troops on parade as they stood to attention. Then the interrogation would begin. This had one terrible problem though. Mr Kent could not say his 'r's and whenever he got really annoyed he would scream into your face:

'I'll bounce you wound this woom like a wubber ball!!!' We couldn't help collapsing into instant hysteria at this point, which unfortunately always led to a worse caning later on!

It was only after I had left school that I realized just how much I had enjoyed it. Despite the many incidents of trouble, and my refusal or inability to get down to work, I had a security and structure there that I was soon to lose.

3

Enter the Supernatural

It is often said that the devil makes work for idle hands and I quickly discovered that there is a lot of truth in this saying. After the initial delight of the summer holiday break and the thought of 'no more boring school lessons', the grim realization that I was going nowhere in my life began to set in. Many of my friends disappeared after the summer holidays and started college or some sort of training scheme. Not me, though. I had no real hobbies or interests and certainly didn't have any desire to go on a training scheme, go to college or get a job. In fact, the very thought of these things filled me with utter dread. I had managed to get some qualifications but most were not of a very high grade (although I did do well in Art and English). I found myself with a lot of time on my hands and I didn't enjoy it.

Evenings and weekends were fine because I would hang out with my friends, but day times were a real problem. I usually lazed about in bed until midday, eventually getting up to potter around the house doing nothing in particular. I spent most of my time watching television and listening to music. At times, I thought I was going out of my mind with boredom, and I constantly seemed to be under my parents' feet. 'Why don't you get a job or something?' my father would frequently demand. But I ignored his suggestion and the underlying frustration which prompted it. I might be bored, but I wasn't *that* bored!

Just to get out of the house, I would often cycle a few miles to Birkenhead Central Library on my father's rattling old bicycle and sit there flicking through the daily newspapers. That was my average day for a number of months; mind-numbingly boring. It was as if someone had pulled a plug and I found myself being sucked down into a whirlpool of monotony and loneliness.

Partly because of my feelings of isolation and lack of direction, I became increasingly aware that there was something missing from my life. In the past, I had often sought to fill this gap by finding solace in dark and mysterious matters and my thoughts naturally began to turn towards them again.

I began to re-evaluate my life and wonder what the meaning of my existence was all about – if indeed there was any real meaning to it. I had plenty of time to ponder this question, and finally came to the conclusion that the average person's lot was to go through school, get a job, get married, have children, and eventually die. The cycle would then be repeated in their children, and their children's children, for ever. This thought bothered me a great deal, and I kept repeating to myself: 'Surely, there must be more to life than this?' I was convinced that there must be an answer to this question, and I needed to find it.

But where? Was there a God? If there was, where was He

and what was He like? Maybe the church could provide me with some answers? But my experiences of church, as a little boy in primary school, didn't encourage me to look for answers there.

Casting my mind back, I remembered a large, cold, stony building where we had to endure long sermons I couldn't understand, from a man with robes on, as we sat on hard uncomfortable pews. Most of the children paid little interest and just messed about, and old women in elaborate hats would turn round and glare at them severely. Even during the singing of the hymns, it seemed that very few people made much of an effort to sing at all, let alone meaningfully. Some just mumbled their way through and my overall impression was that the majority of people didn't even want to be there. I sometimes wondered why they bothered to endure it at all if it was so painful. Certainly, experience had showed that the church couldn't help me in my restless search.

So my quest for answers took me down other paths. I began to look into the world of the paranormal. Browsing through bookshops and newsagents, I felt a strong inner compulsion to purchase literature dealing with strange, unusual and paranormal subjects such as UFOs, ghosts, crop circles and aliens. I had always been fascinated by such topics, and now they provided an escape from the tedium of daily living and maybe even a possible solution to the meaning of this puzzle called life.

Strangely though, after a session immersed in these subjects, I felt as though my personality was being sucked from me and I would become very introverted and reclusive. It seemed that the more I tried to escape into this other world, intriguing though it often was, the more I came away with a dissatisfied, hollow feeling. When I became aware of the effect my studying was having on me, I tried to limit the time I spent reading and thinking about these things. Against my better judgement, however, I was drawn back, time and time again. I still felt convinced that there must be some answers to the meaning of life out there somewhere. Why was the truth so elusive? I was attracted by the enticing possibility that I could unlock some sort of mystical secret and drastically improve my life.

Every book and pamphlet I read about the paranormal was bursting with advertisements, promising all sorts of miracles. 'Revolutionize your life' said one, 'Get money, power and admiration' guaranteed another. One advertisement in particular caught my eye. It was promoting a book on self-improvement. I ordered the book immediately, excited at the prospect it offered of a transformed life.

When the book came I was surprised at some of the techniques that it advised. The author strongly recommended self-hypnosis. I was a bit wary at first, as I had heard some negative things about this practice and was worried that something bad might happen to me. Nevertheless, despite my initial hesitancy, I eventually took the plunge and began practising hypnosis secretly in my bedroom, carefully following the instructions in the book.

Late at night, when everyone else was asleep, I recorded the suggested phrases in what I considered to be a positive and persuasive manner. 'You will succeed in life. You are powerful and will command respect from others.' 'Think rich and you will become rich!' and 'Believe in yourself and you will be successful in life!' Continuing to follow the book's instructions, I rewound the tape, lit a candle and played the tape recording back to myself over and over, while staring at the candle flame. I felt a bit foolish at first, lying there talking to myself, but thought I would give the book a chance, as it promised so much in return (even though the ritual seemed a bit simplistic).

Needless to say, after many weeks of conscientiously following all the instructions in the book to the letter, my life *wasn't* transformed. Probably the only person who had any sort of transformation was the author of the book, whose bank balance must have grown considerably! It left a bitter taste in my mouth as I considered how many others were using his 'tried and tested' methods.

Despite this initial setback in my quest for understanding and self-improvement, I was undeterred. My appetite was whetted by other promises of materialistic fulfilment and spiritual development which caught my eye in the many paranormal magazines I bought. Maybe I had not been bold enough in my early attempts. I decided to try something a bit more complex and mysterious. Advertisements for books on witchcraft and the occult really attracted me, with their air of mystery, thrill and potential. Before long, packages and parcels containing occult spell books were arriving at my home and I began to practise 'white' witchcraft.

The whole idea of witchcraft was hugely appealing to me as a rebellious teenager. For most people, it was an unknown, unacceptable concept; a throwback to murky mediaeval times, nothing to do with the 1980s. The word 'witch' either conjured up a storybook stereotype or someone weird and very alternative.

For example, there was an elderly lady who lived in my

neighbourhood who, because she looked unusual (bent over with a hooked nose), was labelled a witch and consequently harassed by young children on a regular basis. Gangs of them would whip each other up into a frenzy with elaborate stories of the 'terrible things that the witch had done' and descend upon the house of the poor woman, kicking her door and shouting 'Witch! Witch!'

But I scorned such attitudes and indeed exulted in being different and more knowledgeable than the ignorant public. I knew that true witches operated in secret, away from scrutiny, believing that their witchcraft benefited from it. I felt as though I was learning hidden secrets and gaining in-depth spiritual wisdom, accessible only to a few privileged people who were willing to take the time and make the effort to find it. I felt special. My practice of witchcraft seemed harmless enough at the time and there was a new sense of excitement and interest in my life, along with the bonus of the possibility of change for the better.

I set up a secret altar, consisting of candles, a pentagram, and other items of occult paraphernalia, such as parchment, salt and matches in my bedroom. Every day I took it out from its hiding place and performed spells. Many of the spells that I did at this time aimed to satisfy some very basic teenage needs, namely to get extra money and a girlfriend.

One spell involved praying before a full moon and asking for money to come my way. Soon afterwards, as it turned out, I *did* get a job, working for my two uncles at their furniture shop. I attributed the unusual experience of having money in my pocket directly to the success of the magical practices I was involved in. Naturally, this triumph encouraged me to probe more deeply into the world of the occult.

I wanted to learn as much as I possibly could and spent a great deal of time reading occult lore, practice, theory and history. I also began to acquire quite an interesting array of occult accessories, which I proudly set up on the shelves in my bedroom.

Many of the items I put on show consisted of literature about the more recognized and generally more acceptable areas of the occult such as astrology, tarot cards and various aspects of fortune telling. The darker occult books were hidden away because I knew that my parents would be offended and concerned if they saw them. I began to make my own clay models, many of which were extremely grotesque; twisted and tormented faces and creatures with horns, displaying them on my shelves as well. The urge to create such things became almost compulsive. One wall of my bedroom was decorated with a real goat's skull. On the other walls there were eerie posters, one of which was a large black and white montage of screaming demonic faces.

Mum and Dad were not very impressed with my choice of bedroom décor, but put it down to a teenage fad and did no more than roll their eyes in protest. My father was a nominal Catholic, with a respect for the idea of God, even if it wasn't an active belief. He had brought us up to have a traditional understanding of religion, and would not have liked to think that I was getting mixed up in anything 'weird'.

But the more I studied, the more my interest grew and the deeper I descended into the darkest and most esoteric aspects of occultism. I began calling upon spirit entities directly in my spells. One such spell involved getting up very early in the morning, two days running, and reciting certain words in front of large golden candles, to call upon spirits from Egypt. The very words of this spell scared me as they seemed so serious. Despite the gravity of the activity, though, I only did the first half of it, as, in typical teenage fashion, I failed to get out of bed on the second day!

I also attempted 'astral projection' or 'soul travel'. This is the practice of projecting one's spirit or soul out of the body to journey unrestrained by the physical confines of the body and the material world. But despite many attempts to achieve this, my efforts failed completely. The sheer terror of my spirit actually leaving my body caused me to lose all concentration. Also, I had heard much about the possible dangers of this practice, such as the real risk that the spirit would be unable to re-enter the body.

My life had taken on a new dimension. At last, I seemed to have the excitement and purpose I had craved for so long. Yet for all my learning of this new art, I did not understand what was happening to me, and where my activities were leading to. I was obsessed and absorbed by a power beyond my control.

4

Alternative Subculture

Image – what I wore, what I looked like, what music I listened to, who I hung out with – became all-important to me. I wanted to be seen to be different. Dark clothes were a must, reflecting my interest and involvement in the occult. Initially, I leaned towards punk in my style and musical interest. I was into many of the punk bands who were popular in the late 80s, and even some of the original punk bands who were still around from the 70s. I began listening to groups such as GBH, The Exploited, Conflict, the Dead Kennedy's and Crass. Predictably (as their names might hint), these groups had a negative effect on my thinking and attitudes. Most were anti-Christian and anti-establishment, and many of the song lyrics disseminated certain beliefs, world views and political movements such as anarchism and the animal liberation movement. I began to view myself as an anarchist and proudly daubed the anarchy symbol (the letter A with a circle round it) in white paint on the arm of my leather jacket.

I wanted to be with others who shared my beliefs, so began to hang around a shop called Probe Records in Liverpool, as

I had heard this was a popular meeting place for punks and other alternatives. Bona fide record buyers had to brave their way up the large steps leading to the shop, tip-toeing their way through the gangs of mohicans who were sprawled out there, stoned on pot. Despite their fierce appearance however, most of the punks were actually a very friendly bunch and never really caused people any bother.

One of them, perhaps spotting that I was new, made an effort to talk to me, and we became good mates. Joe sported an extremely impressive mohican hairstyle that stood around 14 inches high. He also wore huge Dr Marten boots, and was covered in so many studs and chains that he looked as if he was wearing armour. As we crossed the busy roads of Liverpool city centre, we almost caused accidents, as drivers became distracted by the freakish sight before their eyes.

On one memorable occasion, Joe slept over at our house after we had been to a nightclub called The System. We slept downstairs, draped over the armchair and sofa. The next morning my father came into the room early, not expecting to see anyone there. Joe slowly woke up and got to his feet, still in full armour and with his mohican only a little dented. My father's face was a comical mixture of shock and bemusement as he stared at Joe as if encountering someone from another planet. Without a word, he left the room again, shaking his head in disbelief.

I was never satisfied with one image though and was always looking for something more original and outrageous. Consequently, the punk look quickly transformed into a bizarre, somewhat morbid sort of hybrid of punk and gothic. At the peak of this period in my life, I was dressing in black most of the time, wearing white face paint and black eyeliner! Even though my hair is naturally a very dark brown I always dyed it *jet* black, just to ensure that the look was totally accurate.

I began listening to such groups as Sisters of Mercy, Siouxie and the Banshees, the Cure, and The Mission, but my favourite was a band called Alien Sex Fiend. I loved this group so much that I painted a huge, white, screaming skull on the back of my black biker's leather jacket with the name of the band above it. The shoulders of the jacket were draped in a cobweb-style design and laced with large, spiked studs that were like needles.

Wherever I went, my appearance caused a stir. People who saw me in the street stopped and stared in utter disbelief. Some laughed at me, and some became enraged. I liked the attention, and put up with the jeers; they were worth it to be noticed and different. Only in my home area did I have to be more careful how I looked. There were no Goths, punks or alternatives of any sort in the North End of Birkenhead. People did not take too kindly to the weird and exotic and I knew I would be a target for attack if I wasn't careful. So on days when I knew I would be staying in the immediate area, I toned down my appearance.

Rather to my surprise, my mother actually seemed to like the way I looked. My father, on the other hand, was not so happy. Most of the time he put up with it, but sometimes he was acutely embarrassed by my weird looks, particularly when we were in public, or if he happened to bump into a friend. The only time my father ever became really angry about my appearance was when I pierced my nose with a large stud. I did this by the not-to-be-recommended method of pressing two ice blocks against my nose, then, when it felt numb enough, simply pressing the stud in. Sitting proudly in the living room, I waited for someone to notice. My father kept giving me sideways looks from the other end of the room and eventually asked me about the large spot on my nose. I quickly corrected him and told him it was a nose stud. To my shock, he jumped up angrily and lunged towards me to examine it. He shouted at me to get out of the house and not to come back until 'the b***** thing' was gone. I had no option but to take the stud out.

The weekend was my time to shine. I used to spend most of Friday getting ready for the evening when I went to various nightclubs to meet others in the alternative subculture. On Fridays, I would go to Stairways Nightclub in Birkenhead. This was mostly a club for bikers but was also popular with other subculture groups. I loved the rush of adrenaline and confidence that flooded through me as I walked into the club and headed for the bar to buy my first drink of the night. I knew people were looking me over and saw admiration on their faces. 'And rightly so,' was my response. 'I have put a lot of time and effort into looking like this.' I guess I probably thought a lot of myself at that time!

One of the other clubs I visited regularly was Planet X in Liverpool. Goths, punks, bikers, skinheads, freaks and geeks of every description frequented this dark lair. I found out that, perhaps not surprisingly, many of the alternative people who came to Planet X also had an interest in the occult. Before long, I had made some new friends who shared my interest in music *and* occult spirituality.

Yet despite the busyness, despite the excitement of the clubs and the new-found friendships, I continued to feel very lonely inside. I was often surrounded by people but unable to relate to them in any meaningful way. Communication was usually distant and superficial, often non-existent. Many of the Goths had created such a persona of coolness that they were almost 'too cool' to talk to. They spent entire nights just standing by the bar, like statues, only moving occasionally to flick their long hair back or take a gulp of drink. They seemed soulless, unresponsive and empty. In their attempt to identify with the ultimate dark and mysterious gothic image, they seemed to have lost touch – not only with others around them, but with themselves as well.

But I did have friendships of a kind; travellers down the same paths. Chief among them were Daz and Degsy. Daz was a punk and Degsy was a Goth. Usually, after a late night at Planet X, Degsy and Daz would spend the night at my house, as I was the nearest, and my parents were reasonably tolerant. It was also the most comfortable place to crash. We used to have a lie-in the following day, get up slowly, then spend the rest of the day listening to music and discussing the previous night's events.

One night, much the worse for wear, we staggered into a taxi. The taxi driver looked at us suspiciously but decided not to refuse us.

'Take us to the graveyard!' said Degsy, giggling a little at the odd request.

'That's a new club, isn't it?' said the taxi driver, not liking to admit he didn't know. We shouted with laughter, finding the least thing hilarious.

'No, mate! We mean the *real* graveyard – you know, Flay-brick Cemetery, at the top of Tollemache Road.'

The taxi driver looked at us as if we were mad. 'Why do you want to go there at three o'clock in the morning?' he asked.

'To take some photos of ourselves by the gravestones,' I said, as if it were the most natural thing in the world.

Without another word, the taxi driver took us to the graveyard and deposited us there, leaning out of the window to get a better look. As we leapt over the small cemetery wall, blending rapidly with the enveloping darkness, we heard him shout 'B***** hell!' as he revved up the car and shot off. We posed by the gravestones, the flash of the camera throwing us into brief, eerie relief.

Although Daz and Degsy were better company than most of the other people in the local alternative subculture scene, I only really saw them when we hooked up to go to a night-club – mostly at weekends. During the week, in the evenings, I frequently met up with another group of friends, who were not connected at all with the scene I had got so involved with. Sometimes we hung out in my bedroom listening to music, but much of the time we gathered outside an art gallery in Oxton. A huge gang of us used to sit there, drinking alcohol and making quite a racket – much to the annoyance of the local residents. The police often arrived to move us along as we became a bit of a nuisance.

Soon, alcohol wasn't enough, and we began experimenting with so-called 'soft drugs', mostly in the form of cannabis. This opened up a whole new world for us that we thought was great at the time. We sneaked into the grounds of a nearby dental practice to find a quiet place to smoke pot in a home-made pipe. We then rolled out of the place, falling over each other and laughing like a pack of hyenas, saying ridiculous things like, 'Look, that tree has hundreds of portions of chips on it!' as we made our way back to the art gallery walls, causing yet more commotion for the poor people living nearby.

Thankfully, my experimentation with drugs was relatively minor and I never really liked many of the experiences I had with cannabis. In fact, some of the things that happened were actually quite frightening.

One evening, having already smoked a small amount of potent pot, I set off with some friends to a local pub. By the time we reached it, we were all laughing hysterically. Gradually, though, the intensity of the drug began to escalate until it became too unpleasant to bear. One of my friends noticed the look on my face and said, 'Look! He's on a downer!' Frightened, I didn't know what to do, so followed them into the pub. I felt as if everyone in it was staring at me and I sank, trembling, into a chair. Severe claustrophobia and panic rose in me. I had to get out! My legs were like jelly as I staggered to the door, and I was convinced that the entire pub was laughing at me.

The park was the quickest and most familiar route to safety. Now though, it was a place of fear and danger. Large matchstick-shaped people loomed at me by the trees. I ran but I could only run in slow motion. I finally made it through to the end of the second park and could see the gate in view, with the welcoming street lights glowing beyond. Encouraged by the sight, I put my head down and ran as hard as I could. But to my horror, I suddenly saw a gang of about thirty people blocking the way to freedom. I closed my eyes for a second; when I opened them, they had all disappeared! The relief, when I finally got home, was enormous. It took some time to recover, and needless to say I decided not to go any further down the drug-taking path, and even became quite 'anti-pot'; a view which earned the displeasure of some of my friends who enjoyed smoking the drug. I was much more comfortable drinking alcohol and equipped myself with a generous supply of gin or vodka when we gathered round the art gallery.

As the weeks went by, rumours of our unofficial get-together spread on the local youth grapevine. Every night, someone new would join us, often from quite a distance, via a friend, relative, or work colleague. The crowd became quite big and raucous, thus attracting even more local teenagers, and though police and residents tried to be diplomatic in their approach, it was obvious that the situation could not continue much longer without trouble.

5

Youth Club

One evening, as a few of the gang were sitting quietly before the crowd arrived, a small lady with short, blonde hair approached. Braving our stares and mutters, she marched up to us all, introduced herself as Jackie and said, 'Don't you all get bored sitting around here with nothing to do all the time?' We agreed that it *was* boring but that there was nowhere for us to go. She went on, 'How would you feel about coming to our youth club? It's just down the road next to St Mark's Church. We have got darts, pool and a snack shop? Why not come along?'

We looked at each other enquiringly, with much shrugging of shoulders, and finally someone asked, 'When does it start?' 'Right now, if you want to come along,' she replied. So we all trooped down the road to the small building adjoining the large and very old Anglican church of St Mark.

We walked into a shabby, echoing, sparsely equipped hall, occupied by a couple of teenagers playing pool, and half a dozen nervous-looking adults. Jackie brightly made a general introduction and encouraged us to make ourselves at home. There wasn't a great deal to engage us, yet the evening turned out to be quite enjoyable. We played pool, darts and table tennis and consumed the drinks and biscuits on offer. Some of the helpers were visibly taken aback at how loud and unruly some of the gang were and maintained a cautious distance, smiling rigidly whenever they made eye contact with us. But despite this rather shaky start, we all decided that we would return the following week. After all, it beat sitting on a wall, shivering in the cold!

Although the people who ran the youth club were Christians, we were pleased to find that they didn't rant on about God. Instead, they made it clear that they were Christians through their actions. Occasionally, one or other of them would drop something into a conversation about their faith in a non-threatening manner. This was my first positive introduction to the Christian religion, though I thought nothing of it. We liked having something different to do, and put up with the leaders, but behind their backs, we mocked them, calling them geeky Bible bashers.

On our way home from the youth club, we used to walk through Birkenhead Park, stopping on the way sometimes. On one such occasion, one of our gang took the opportunity to entertain us by imitating an American-style TV evangelist. He was particularly good at doing impersonations and put on a very animated display to his 'audience' seated on the grass. In his best effort at an American accent he declaimed, 'I tell you brothers and sisters that *now* is the time to repent! Can I hear an amen?' To this we all gleefully responded, 'Amen, brother! You preach it!' Even though I was hysterical with laughter, I suddenly became quite uneasy when my friend began mocking the name of Jesus over and over again. I couldn't put my finger on why I felt this way, but knew in my heart that he had overstepped a boundary. Not wanting to look the odd one out, I continued laughing. But now the laughter was forced and hollow as I kept up the pretence. When the hilarity eventually died down, I was left with an uncomfortable, guilty feeling, though I couldn't work out why I felt this way. We walked away from the blasphemous scene to our separate homes. I felt stained inside.

Jackie and the others who ran the St Mark's youth club had a lot to put up with when they opened their doors to our motley crew. They knew that we sometimes came into the club high on either alcohol or drugs and that we were often quite disruptive and rude. But despite our challenging behaviour, they were patient and considerate towards us and we continued to experience Christianity in action through them. Sometimes we saw them sitting quietly, talking about us. Little did we know that they were actually praying for us.

Because of their kindness, they eventually won our trust and respect, and became good friends and positive role models in a world that seemed to have no moral boundaries. They always had a listening ear and friendly advice. To those of us who did ask questions about God, they were happy to respond. Many a night was spent with one or more of the group having an in-depth discussion in a quiet corner of the youth club hall. I, however, stayed well clear of such cosy chats. 'I like them, and sort of respect their views,' I reasoned to myself, 'but the boring religious talk is not for me, thank you very much.' I continued to keep my distance from them.

Despite my reluctance to engage in conversations about religion, I did occasionally take the youth group leaders up on their invitations to attend some of the church services. We went for a laugh and a change of activity, and sat on the hard pews, sniggering at the unusual setting we found ourselves in. We would also whisper humorous and imaginative running commentaries to each other about what we thought was, or should be, happening. Regular church members would glare at us as we unsuccessfully tried to suppress the laughter that was infecting us all. At the end of the service, we had no understanding of anything that had been said or done and were even more scornful of those who seemed to take it so seriously. Our youth club leaders, meanwhile, were plainly embarrassed by our shameful performance.

Yet still they didn't give up on us, and took us on various days out, such as a walk in the countryside, bowling or ice skating. Sometimes we went to religious events as well. A memorable occasion was a trip to Chester, where there were lots of other youth groups meeting at the racecourse. As I looked about, I saw vicars playing football with young people and noticed how many of these young people seemed different to our lot. They were much more respectful, for a start, and also they seemed to be far happier and enthusiastic than we were.

As we waited, wondering why we were really there, our own vicar, whom we called 'Nick the Vic', outlined the day's events to us. Nick told us that the plan was for lots of youth clubs to meet up together and then march through the city of Chester, each displaying our respective banners identifying which area we were from. He enthusiastically waved aloft a banner with 'Birkenhead' emblazoned on it. Our destination at the end of the march was a nearby church where there would be a service. Nick told us that if we behaved ourselves at the service, we would then be going to an outdoor rock concert behind the church.

We quickly took up our places, which, because they were in alphabetical order, meant that we were at the front of the march, behind the Bishop of Chester. He looked a bit nervous as we all filed in eagerly behind him and he had every reason to be so, as he couldn't have been prepared for what was ahead of him. The other youth groups took their place behind us and the march began. Like an invading army in a foreign land, we proudly held our Birkenhead banner high. We took the opportunity to jeer at the local Chester gangs as we walked past them in the town centre, which caused them to sneer and launch insults back at us. The poor bishop soldiered on with a jostling, disruptive, swearing mob behind him. When there were no bystanders to threaten or make faces at anymore, our attention turned to the bishop himself. My friend nudged me and, pointing at the bishop's long flowing robe, spat at it. I copied this, as did the others. We thought the whole thing was hysterical. The bishop himself appeared to be unaware of what we had done, or, more likely, he just chose to ignore our behaviour altogether.

We soon arrived at the church and, as usual, sniggered and whispered all the way through, paying no attention to what was being said. After the service, we were ushered out through a side door into a large garden. There was a platform with drums, microphones and guitars and a group of spandex-clad long-haired men pottering around. We found ourselves a comfortable spot by a hedge near the back of the garden, not too close, just in case something 'weird' was going to happen.

The band started up and, much to my surprise, they were very good. The music they played was really cool rock. I didn't listen to the lyrics too much but one of our friends, Dave, was listening intently. While we were all smiling, his face was like thunder. The lead singer of the group was speaking between one of the songs and said, 'We serve a great God! I want to thank the Lord Jesus Christ for giving us the gift of music!' At this, Dave, who had been looking increasingly annoyed throughout, sprang to his feet and shouted a tirade of obscenities while shaking his fist at the band. The speaker carried on talking, but was looking over to where we were sitting, perhaps a bit distracted by the continuing interruption.

Jackie managed to calm Dave down a little and he sat down, seething like a boiling inferno. Eventually, he got up again and stormed off to a nearby pub. After the concert had finished he reappeared, seemingly unconcerned about his earlier behaviour. I, on the other hand, was totally shocked by it! I couldn't fathom why he had reacted so violently. I was also extremely embarrassed by what had happened, particularly as he was sitting right next to me. I felt very sorry for the band, who didn't deserve that sort of treatment.

On the whole, we all really enjoyed the day. It tore down some of the stereotypes we had of Christians generally, and encouraged us to keep going to the youth group at St Mark's.

6

Darren

'Don't look now, but you wouldn't believe what's come to join us!' muttered Jimmy, none too quietly. 'Looks a bit weird, don't he?'

I looked up from the pool table and stared at the tall, thin newcomer. He was wearing a rather strange, large and heavy army trench coat, with a shirt, smart trousers and a blazer underneath. A striking contrast to the normal teenage uniform of scruffy jeans and sweatshirts. He stood quietly, looking rather nervous. Jackie bustled up to introduce him.

'This is Darren. He's Derek's son, but he doesn't know anyone here. Make him welcome, boys!'

Derek was one of the youth workers at St Mark's youth club. We grunted a greeting to Darren, but he seemed a bit wary of us and stayed close to the youth workers. During his first few visits, he kept a safe distance and helped out in the background, with the snack shop.

Gradually though, Darren did come out of himself a bit

and began to mix more with the rest of the youth group. He turned out to be quite a fascinating character, well spoken, witty, intelligent and a good conversationalist. I became particularly good friends with him and, to my delight, discovered that despite being from a Christian family, he shared my interest in witchcraft and the occult.

As our friendship grew, Darren and I spent much time together experimenting with spells and seeking ways to improve our spiritual knowledge and abilities. As well as spell-casting, we practised such things as tarot cards, palm reading, creating talismans, astral projection, hypnosis, telekinesis and telepathy. We also browsed through book-shops, looking for books on the occult, and used to get together to compare notes. As practitioners of witchcraft, we were proud to call ourselves witches, though I've since discovered that this title means many things to many people.

We didn't hide our hobby from the youth group, and indeed took delight in frightening some of the people there by pointedly mentioning some of the occult activities that we had been involved in. Whenever I bought a drink, I made sure that I paid with the hand that sported a five-pointed pentagram star ring; a popular symbol of witch-craft. The look of shock on their faces as they recognized the ring caused me great satisfaction.

People just didn't know how to respond to us. In fact, there were even some who seemed visibly afraid of us. These kind, caring Christians were ill-equipped to deal with the dangers Darren and I were plunging into. They were obviously deeply concerned about our behaviour, yet no one ever challenged me about it. I knew that Darren's parents had warned him many times about his occult involvement, but he ignored them.

It was great to have a friend who shared my interest, yet I began to have stirrings of unease about him. My first visit to his bedroom was a shock, for I quickly discovered that, despite his clean and well-dressed appearance, Darren did not apply the same standards to his accommodation. His parents' home, a large middle floor flat, was nicely kept, but as we tried to enter his room, the door was jammed by something. When we eventually forced our way in, I saw that the obstruction was a heap of stones, soil and gravel that had been spilt on the floor. There was rubbish all over the floor – plant pots turned upside down and broken, smashed records, paper everywhere, sweet wrappers, dirty crockery. We crunched over the concealed carpet, crushing plastic, glass and various other unknown items under our feet. It is true that teenagers are not the most tidy of people, and I certainly fell into that category myself, but I had never seen a room as messy as this. I was particularly shocked because of the contrast with Darren's personal fastidiousness.

I stood gaping at the chaos, unable to take in the rest of the room, only dimly aware of the bed and other furniture and various posters on the wall. Darren, meanwhile, seemed oblivious to the effect that his room was having on me, and proudly drew my attention to a large hole that had been knocked through at the top of his cupboard. Abruptly, he hoisted himself up into the cupboard and inching his way up towards the hole, he clambered through it and disappeared into the darkness. As I peered upwards, his face suddenly reappeared and he said, 'Come on up! I have something to show you.'

Somewhat hesitantly, I followed him up and found myself in the attic of the house, lit only by a torch. I was expecting to see something interesting, but all that was up there was a chair and a few household items. It was dirty, dark and cold. I asked Darren what he did here. He pointed at the chair, 'Oh, I often sit here for hours, meditating alone.' This was the point when I began to realize that there was a lot I didn't really know about Darren.

Yet despite this disquiet, our friendship continued. In our quest for spirituality we did some pretty stupid things at times. On one occasion we were talking about mind over matter and how eastern 'holy men' were able to endure walking over hot coals. Darren told me that he was able to hold a lighted match against his hand, and through the power of his mind, not feel any pain whatsoever. He asked me if I would like to have a go and managed to persuade me that I wouldn't feel any pain as long as I believed it wouldn't hurt me. Dazzled by his bravado, I foolishly agreed. It never occurred to me to ask him for a demonstration first! He lit the match, immediately placed it, flame first, into my outstretched hand, and eagerly stood back to watch my reactions. I really tried hard to convince myself that it would not hurt, and for a moment, it didn't seem to. Then suddenly, I felt an excruciating pain in the palm of my hand, causing me to yelp like a wounded dog! Darren had an expression of glee on his face as I tried to be cool about it and made out that it wasn't a problem. But I was badly burnt and within a short time a large painful bubble appeared on my palm. I bandaged it but kept aggravating the injury when I picked things up.

Darren also prided himself in being able to read the tarot cards and I noticed that he did seem to have a professionalism about him as he talked people through the meaning of the cards. Once, when he was reading my cards, he seemed particularly disturbed at what he saw. As he turned card after card over he told me that he kept getting the impression that there was someone, or something, intent on bringing me down. 'It's like the knives are out,' he said. 'Something bad is going to happen to you.' At the time, neither of us realized the chilling accuracy of his prediction. My progressively serious involvement in the occult had opened a door through which hostile spiritual forces were able to pursue me and cause my ruin.

Inevitably, perhaps, my relationship with Darren began to deteriorate. We came to a phase where we always seemed to be in competition with each other, causing a lot of tension, suspicion and jealousy. Once, when we had a sharp disagreement about the best way to perform a particular spell, Darren, perhaps in an effort to win the argument, made a startling confession. 'I have been watching what you get up to in private, when I astrally project my spirit out of my body!' I turned round, horrified at what he had said, looking at him with a mixture of shock and anger. He responded by shooting me a scary, wide-eyed sideways glance, which made me think, 'This guy is totally nuts!' I knew then that I needed to draw our strange relationship to a close.

Whenever I saw Darren after this, he was displaying increasingly bizarre behaviour. One day, for instance, I was waiting at the bus stop over the road from my home when I looked down to St James Church and noticed Darren standing alone in the church grounds. He was wearing his familiar trench coat and was, as usual, quite smartly dressed. However, he had gone even further on this occasion and was wearing a bright red dickey-bow tie. He pretended not to see me at first, but then acknowledged my presence and walked up to greet me. I asked him what he had been doing and he told me that he had been sitting in the grounds for many hours, meditating alone and smoking a cigar.

I was genuinely worried that he actually could spy on me secretly through 'astral projection' or 'soul travel', which made me very edgy when I was alone in my room. I did feel as if I was being watched. Was it just my imagination, or was there some truth to what Darren had said? I just could not brush off these doubts, and so began to acquire books that demonstrated how to carry out spells of protection from prying astral spies.

After a while, our friendship died a natural death. Darren came less and less frequently to the youth club, and we didn't spend any time together otherwise. Eventually, he stopped coming altogether and I didn't hear from him again. News did filter through, however, that he had trashed the vicar's house and left tarot cards and occult paraphernalia everywhere. When we pressed the leaders of the youth club for more information, they were hesitant to give any, other than to add that some of the other things that he had done were so vile that they felt they had no other option but to involve the police. Darren and his family moved away from the area soon afterwards.

Overall, I was greatly relieved to be free of him, but a little part of me was sad, as he had been the only person with whom I could share my interest in the world of the occult and paranormal.

7
Changes

The room was dim and gloomy, with flickering candles sending the grotesque figures and skulls on the shelves into sinister relief. Shadows traced an eerie dance on the walls and an acrid smoke permeated the air. The group huddled round the table, staring as if hypnotised at the cards I was turning over. The atmosphere crackled with an inexplicable force. I turned over the next card and recoiled.

'It's the death card!' I proclaimed dramatically. The others gasped and at that precise moment there was a huge crash and the glass shelf just above us smashed to the ground, scattering its load of occult ornaments. Everyone screamed and clutched each other in fear. I leapt to switch the light on and, trembling, we surveyed the damage. The explanation soon became clear; a burning candle underneath had cracked the shelf, causing it to shatter.

But the coincidence of the accident with the appearance of the death card was the final straw for my friends. They were already concerned by my increasingly weird appearance and behaviour. They didn't like my room or the books

I was reading. They were scared by my tales of spells and other odd practices. They preferred the comfort of normal teenage rebellion.

I suddenly found myself alone . . . a lot! This, combined with unemployment again, meant that I had a great deal of spare time on my hands. My reaction was defiance – 'Right, I will throw myself even more into gaining more knowledge about the occult and obtain power, riches and respect. That will show them!' So, like a dedicated scientist, I pursued my goals, ordering even more occult-related books from various suppliers. And as my quest for power and deeper spiritual understanding continued, my studies became more and more sinister and malevolent.

Every night, and often during the day as well, I experimented with all sorts of combinations of the occult in my bedroom, taking spells from books, changing them and mixing them with my own material. My parents continued to be unaware of what I was getting up to, although they must have suspected *something* because of my secretiveness and the many unusual packages that came to the house through the post. They never asked me what these parcels were but I could tell that they desperately wanted to know. But I ignored their unspoken pleas and fobbed them off with a lie before locking myself in my room again.

I was lonely, though. I hated to admit it, but I missed my friends. All the pleasure I gained at my progress in the occult was spoiled by my isolation. I began to get depressed.

One evening, alone as usual in my bedroom, I heard a familiar voice in the street outside. I edged slowly towards my bedroom window, not wanting to be seen, and saw a group of about five of my friends heading towards my house. 'Company, at last!' I thought happily. Then my heart sank as they walked right past my house, without so much as a glance, and called on Mark instead, who lived a couple of doors down from me. 'They are probably calling for him first,' I thought, and eagerly watched and waited for them to call on me next. But when they eventually emerged, they walked right past my house again, apparently without any thought of me. I felt deeply hurt and angry that my new activities and interests had driven my friends away.

This incident made me realize afresh how much I was missing my friends and prompted me to make a radical decision. I decided that in order to be accepted again, I would have to go 'underground' with my occult activities. I would tell my mates that I was no longer going to have anything to do with such things as witchcraft, tarot cards, or the paranormal, but at the same time I would continue my studies and practice in greater secrecy. For their benefit as well, I slowly shed the gothic image and started to dress more normally again. I took the initiative and began to call on them. My friends were cautious at first and seemed very apprehensive of me. I knew I had scared them with my interest in the occult, but I didn't realize until this point just *how much* I had scared them. Some of them were extremely frightened by the changes they had seen in me and the strange things that had been happening. Slowly though, they received me back into the fold.

One of my friends suggested I join them in the pubs and clubs they frequented in Birkenhead rather than the dark gothic nightclubs that I had been haunting for so long. Wanting to please I readily agreed, and from then on I went regularly to nightclubs and pubs around the Birkenhead area, often getting exceedingly drunk. The camaraderie of those days was very rewarding. Despite the alcoholic blur, I have fond memories of deep friendships, loyalty and laughter. But I lived a double life. In private, I was still very much involved with my dark interests, as my quest to understand more of the occult world continued under a veil of shadowy secrecy.

My restored social life gave me a fresh impetus in considering my future. I realized that I needed to get some qualifications to make me more employable. Previous experience of government training schemes had left me disillusioned and reluctant to try again. But I admitted to myself that maybe I had not been as committed as I might have been. This time, I looked for something which I would actually enjoy and follow through.

My search eventually led me to an art and design training organization called Apex, situated above a furniture shop in Rock Ferry. The course was very casual and informal, comprising a mixture of painting, drawing and photography. It wasn't long before I settled in and began to make new friends. To my delight, I discovered that many of the trainees were Goths and punks and I returned thankfully to my black clothes, glad to conform with this new environment.

It was fun on the training scheme, but we didn't actually *do* very much. In fact, one lad sat reading a book every day without being asked to stop. The course leaders didn't really seem to care about the trainees and didn't give us much guidance or challenge. Many of the trainees were there simply to get an extra ten pounds on top of their benefits and to get the Job Centre off their backs. Some went to the photography dark-room to smoke pot, while others were on harder drugs. The course tutors knew of this but simply turned a blind eye.

One of the trainees was a known heroin addict. He spent most of his day in the canteen area chatting and smoking cigarettes. Even though we all knew he struggled with a serious drug problem, we rarely discussed his habit. Gradually though, it became impossible to ignore the effect that it was having on him. He began to look more and more worn down; his face gaunt, grey and deathly. One day, as he was sitting in the canteen, crouched over with his head in his hands, I asked him if he was OK, at which he looked up and said, in a voice of total misery and desperation, 'Vince, I just want to get off the gear [slang for heroin].' I will never forget the look of utter torment and hopelessness in his eyes.

There were also a lot of bizarre and colourful characters at Apex. One punk used to ask people if he could buy their souls. People thought that it was a joke until he offered them money (I think £5.00 was the going rate!). Of course, when people realized that he was actually *serious*, most declined his offer fairly rapidly. But others, who saw it as a quick way of making easy money, agreed and took the payment. After collecting a number of names on pieces of paper, he told us that he put them in a small cardboard box and burnt them! He never explained, though, *why* he did this.

One of the Goths was teased unmercifully about the exceptional paleness of his skin. He was constantly being asked if he used white make-up, or if he was in training to be a clown or a mime. He strenuously denied the make-up allegation and maintained that his complexion was natural.

We wondered why this 'natural' complexion had so many white streaks and lines under the chin and along the jaw line!

Even though I was meant to be training towards employment, my time at Apex just became one big social event. Life was enjoyable but I was going nowhere. It was a carefree lull before a violent storm which would turn my existence upside down.

8

Jane

The knock on the door startled us, but gave no premonition of the huge changes it would herald in all our lives. My parents looked at each other in mild surprise and my father heaved himself to his feet to answer it. Mum and I strained our ears to make out the voices and then Dad came back in, nodding me to the door. 'Someone for you,' he grunted, adding, 'don't know who,' to my raised eyebrows. Mystified, I went to the door and saw two ladies standing there.

They looked nervously at each other, presumably waiting for the other to speak. A small, middle-aged lady with short, dark red hair and a soft Welsh accent spoke first. She introduced herself as the mother of Jane and the other lady as her aunt. They explained that they had come because Jane was in a local mental health ward and had been asking for me. She had suffered some sort of breakdown, they explained, and I was the only person she wanted to see. My mind raced; Jane and I had had a brief relationship around eight months ago, and now she was asking for me! I had been quite attracted to her, but sadly it didn't seem to be reciprocated, because the relationship had fizzled out after a short while.

What particularly encouraged me was that just after we were last together, I cast a number of 'love spells' in the hope of getting Jane back. They didn't seem to work, so I eventually gave up and tried to forget about her. Now, a few months later, here she was asking for me. 'It worked after all!' I congratulated myself elatedly. 'It really did work!'

Spurred on by the apparent success of my spell casting, within a few days I took up the invitation to visit Jane. I stood at the entrance of a large open area in the hospital and scanned what seemed to be a large number of residents. Some were quietly reading, some were having conversations with one another, and others seemed agitated and paced up and down muttering to themselves.

Jane was crouched by a record player, withdrawn and nervous like a timid animal. Her petite prettiness had an air of fragility and she was strikingly pale. Her white face was framed by long black hair and black clothes, so that she looked almost ghostly. She stood up as I made my way towards her and smiled in welcome, saying how embarrassed she was to be seen in this state, but that she really needed a friend at this time. I was flattered that she had thought of *me* in this way. She seemed so anxious and vulnerable and I felt very sorry for her. As she talked and talked, I realized that she had been through a lot of misery and pain.

At first, I went once a week to the hospital. Then, more often, at Jane's request. I didn't mind, because it was obvious that she benefited from my visits, becoming more lively and less withdrawn. I was on a mission to bring her back to health, and in my flush of goodwill I didn't notice at the time that she was actually quite manipulative and demand-ing. Sometimes when I needed to leave, she used a variety of tactics to persuade me to stay, such as physically holding on to me, making me feel guilty, or becoming very moody. I sensed that she was very jealous of me spending any time with other friends, but put it down to her fragile state of mind.

'Just to let you know that she's been discharged,' boomed Jane's dad down the phone, 'so don't bother going up there.'

'But . . . is she ready?' I faltered, shifting uncomfortably from foot to foot in the shop where I was making the call on my mobile, hoping people couldn't hear.

'No, probably not, but they won't have her there any more. She's been trashing the place again.'

Jane had lost control and smashed up crockery, vases, even furniture in the ward. Her violence was such that it took a couple of charge nurses to overpower her, and there were fears that she might have become violent with other patients. This was not the first outburst, and I was told that the hospital had decided that they could not keep her there any longer. I didn't question the decision, nor query whether it was wise to allow someone apparently that dis-turbed to live in the community with no support.

But I was astounded to hear the news. Jane was undoubtedly strange, but she had never given any sign of violent tendencies. The descriptions of her behaviour in the hospital seemed to belong to another person entirely. I comforted myself with the belief that she would never behave like that with me. I was a good influence on her, after all.

With Jane's return to her parents' bungalow in Leasowe, a new phase began in my life. She seemed to need me more and more and eventually I was virtually living there; spending most of each day at the bungalow and often sleeping there as well. We occupied our time watching videos, listening to music or browsing round the local shopping centre. I saw very little of my parents and friends and no longer hung out at the local pubs and clubs. To the outside world, we must have seemed like a couple besotted with each other, but the strange thing was that we were not actually boyfriend and girlfriend in the established sense. We had no physical relationship – I did try to kiss her once but she did not respond and I didn't try again – and did not have an emotional closeness either. She seemed simply to want someone who would be a friend and take care of her. I lived in hope that as her mental health improved, so would the quality of our relationship.

But I missed my friends and family, and though I liked to be needed and usually enjoyed spending time with Jane, I also needed a break from her occasionally. Often, I was extremely drained by her erratic, intense behaviour and demanding attitudes. I didn't want to end our friendship, merely to see a bit less of each other. However, when I expressed this to her, she reacted quite strongly, clinging on to me and pleading with me emotionally, 'Don't you want to be with me? I really feel afraid to sleep tonight. You make me feel safe and wanted. *Please* stay and watch over me.' When I hesitated, she changed tack, and became quite flirtatious, playing on my obvious attraction to her. I gave in and, not wanting to upset or anger her, I put my own life on hold and continued to support her. But as time went on, I began to feel more and more trapped, as if I was being emotionally suffocated.

At the same time, Jane was growing in confidence in her own power in the relationship. Her behaviour changed subtly, to the point where she was controlling almost everything that I did. Any suggestions I made, whether about the day's activities, or videos to watch, or even the food we might eat were challenged, ridiculed or dismissed out of hand and her choices substituted. Because these things seemed quite trivial, I didn't want to cause a fuss over them, and so Jane had her way in everything.

I was surprised to discover that Jane was extremely interested, and even proficient, in the occult. She encouraged me to continue my own practice in it and we performed spells together. To my dismay and embarrassment, she made a special point of telling her parents that I was interested in the subject. I really felt as though she had put me on the spot and was in no position to deny the things I thought I had shared with her in confidence. She spoke quite brazenly about some of the occult activities I was involved in, apparently with the intention of frightening them. She smiled in triumph as her parents (who were nominal Catholics) squirmed uncomfortably.

Then came the time when I saw for myself the violence I had found so hard to believe of her. It was triggered by her parents, rather than by me, but was nonetheless very distressing to witness. Although many young people have arguments with their parents, this went far beyond the norm. If Jane wanted something, particularly money, she used to ask her parents over and over again, apparently in an attempt to wear them down. They were obviously accustomed to playing this game with her. Sometimes, they gave way to the pressure but on this particular occasion they refused. Undeterred, she continued the mantra of 'Can I have some money?' When this method failed she switched tactics to emotional blackmail, saying such things as 'I thought you loved me'. She kept this up until the realization dawned that she had been unsuccessful. That was when she flew into a rage, screaming, shouting and damaging anything within her immediate vicinity. Cups, plates, ornaments, crashed around the room, as she tore around like a tornado demolishing everything in her path.

I stood motionless, totally shocked by the outburst, longing to be elsewhere. Jane's mother was screaming and crying, her father was trying vainly to stop the violence. Finally, she came to a halt, panting with exertion and surveyed the havoc she had created. I was flushed with embarrassment, but she didn't seem affected. When her father started ranting at her, she slammed out of the room, leaving us to clear up the mess. Jane's mother was sobbing uncontrollably and her father, muttering imprecations, abruptly left the house, presumably to seek solace at the local pub. We could hear Jane still shrieking and swearing in her room, and it was hours before she eventually emerged and grudgingly offered an apology. Scenes like this became all too familiar as the months progressed.

Being a Goth, I was no stranger to morbid things, but Jane took the topic further than I was comfortable with. She was fascinated by death, talking about it incessantly and drawing ghoulish pictures. She also loved watching horror films. The only room with a video recorder was the front living room. This was Jane's mother's 'showroom' and we were only allowed to view videos in there; we were not allowed to smoke, eat, or drink. During our time in the showroom, we watched such horror films as *Children of the Corn*, *The Fog*, *Hellraiser* and one that we repeatedly watched, *The Lost Boys*, a film about gothic teenage vampires who rode motorbikes. Jane was obsessed with watching films like this. Often, I noticed that her attention was as much on me as on the film. She waited for my reaction to the scenes that were the most disturbing and then lit up with delight if I reacted in shock or disgust.

The full extent of her morbid interest became apparent after the Hillsborough football disaster in 1989 when 96 people were tragically crushed to death. Jane's father was at the football match that day, and as reports began to filter through in the form of newsflashes on the television, we started to panic. We had no way of knowing if Jane's dad was one of the victims and could only wait for more news. Jane's mother became more and more disturbed and frantic as the terrible details and images poured into the living room. In contrast, Jane seemed excited, exhilarated even, by the whole event. Her behaviour really jarred, because it seemed so unnatural to act in such a way, especially when her own father could well be one of the fatalities.

As we waited tensely, we heard a door slam and Jane's father came into the room. Her mother ran to him and embraced him, crying tears of relief. He was ashen-faced and shaking as he walked silently to his chair. The haunted expression on his face, coupled with the reports we had seen on the television, were enough for us to understand that he had been through a horrific experience and was suffering from shock. Jane, though, didn't seem to care about her father's feelings, nor did she express any relief that he was safe. All she seemed interested in was finding out the grisly details of the deaths, asking him question after question about how people died, what they looked like, how they sounded.

Over the following days and weeks, Jane continued to follow the disaster with interest. She collected an array of newspaper articles on the subject. One in particular made a big impression on me. The photograph showed the appalling image of a group of fans trapped behind the wire fence just before they were crushed to death. One man had long hair and a beard. His face held a look of impending doom and despair, as though he knew that this was going to be the end for him. It was dreadful; a look of utter hopelessness. Jane carried this article around with her. She kept showing the picture to people, pointing particularly to the man with the beard and saying, 'Look. Don't you think this man looks like Jesus?'

9

Demons

The day had started with such high expectations. Jane's parents had set off for a week's much-needed holiday, leaving me to look after their daughter. I got on reasonably well with them, for even though they obviously considered me a bit weird, they seemed to think that I was generally a positive influence on their daughter. I felt pleased that they trusted me to be in charge while they were away. We had said our goodbyes and gone into Birkenhead shopping centre for a few hours.

I expected Jane to be happy and relieved at the prospect of being free of her parents for an entire week, but instead, she seemed particularly anxious. On several occasions, I noticed her gazing blankly just above my head. Seeing my uneasiness, she said, 'I can see something like a white cloud hovering above your head.' I laughed it off, thinking she was joking. But she was not laughing.

On our return to the empty house, I produced a bottle of vodka, looking forward to a good night. Despite my high spirits, I did have a niggle of concern, as Jane's behaviour had become increasingly strange as the day wore on. But I quickly dismissed my worries with the reminder that her mental health problems made it inevitable that she would have some days when she would struggle. I was used to her highs and lows by this time.

All of a sudden, Jane stood up and began pacing up and down the kitchen talking very quickly. It was hard to make out what she was saying; the words seemed to burst out from her almost uncontrollably. At first I thought she was attempting to entertain me with some humorous impersonations, and laughed encouragingly. But as she continued to pace up and down, speaking faster and faster, almost to the point of hysteria, I became alarmed. 'OK, you can stop that now, it's not funny anymore.' She was oblivious to my protests, waving her arms about as she gabbled on and on. I thought she must be having some sort of mental breakdown, and wondered whether I should call the doctor. Then, abruptly, she stopped and slumped down at the kitchen table. She fixed me with her eyes, piercing me with a look of sheer hate and contempt and started to speak.

The voice was not hers, yet it was coming from her mouth; a deep, male tone, speaking ugly, hateful words in an odd dialect. Her movements and mannerisms didn't belong to her either. It was as if she had become a completely different person before my very eyes. I was frozen in fear and horror. My instinct was to flee, but I could not move. For that moment, I was actually paralysed, unable to do anything except watch and listen to the scene in front of me.

I could not make out all the opening words, but I clearly heard it speak about Jane as though she wasn't even present. In fact, there was a point when it was obvious that I was no longer talking to Jane. It wasn't just her voice that changed. Her whole personality seemed to have undergone a drastic transformation. Memories of my many studies in demonology and the occult flooded into my mind as I pointed at the character before me and said, almost excitedly, 'I know what you are! You are a demon aren't you?' The voice agreed. 'There are good demons and bad demons. I am a good demon.' I should have remembered that they are also master liars.

The voice professed to be that of a spirit who had inhabited Jane since early childhood. It threatened to kill me and everyone I cared about if I told anyone of its existence. It boasted that it had the supernatural power to do this and asked me if I would like to see an example of the things it was capable of doing. I was absolutely petrified and my gut reaction was to run out of the house and back to my parents' home. I tried edging towards the door, but Jane was too quick for me. She unleashed a stream of curses and threats, including that of death to me and my family. I was trapped in the kitchen, with no alternative but to remain and talk to this spirit.

We talked right through the night until the light crept through the curtains and I heard the birds singing outside. This spirit declared that the reason for Jane's mental health problems was because of its presence, but it further revealed that its time had now come to leave her. Before leaving, it said that I was never to abandon Jane because I had been 'chosen' to look after her. With this, Jane lay on the settee, closed her eyes for a few minutes, then sprang up full of energy. She acted as though she had no recollection of the events of the previous night and seemed to be her usual self. In contrast, I was exhausted, physically, mentally and emotionally.

Later on that afternoon, though still preoccupied with the strange encounter of the previous night, I was just starting to come to terms with all that had happened. I began to have hope that it was all over. After all, the spirit had said that it was leaving, and that I was to look after Jane. It had been a terrible experience, but it was finished. As I turned to tell her my thoughts, I saw to my horror that her face had assumed the same arrogant and contemptuous look that had preceded the terror yesterday. Cruel eyes pinned me to my seat with their gaze. This was accompanied by the voice I had talked with for so long into the early hours of that morning. My heart froze, my mouth went dry, and I felt as though I was falling backwards into a void. Frightened and dismayed, I mustered up the courage to say something. In a feeble voice I faltered, 'I thought you had gone.' The voice replied mockingly, 'I lied.' This time, the spirit seemed even more threatening and suggested that I had not carried out some of the instructions it had previously commanded me. For this reason, it told me, it had to remain to ensure that I complied with all that was expected of me. There was to be no end to my ordeal.

As the week progressed, more and more spirits became evident. There was no pattern to these appearances. We could be out shopping or in the house, watching television or eating a meal. One minute Jane was herself, the next she was a different person. As each day passed, the spirits appeared more frequently, sometimes with gaps of time between, sometimes one after the other in rapid succession. Each spirit was distinguishable by its voice and by the varying actions and gestures Jane made. Some were strange and mysterious, some were strong and intimidating and some were even humorous at times. It seemed as if each spirit had a different persona. It was extremely hard to know where Jane was in the midst of all these characters jostling for dominance. But after a while, I began to realize that she did have some awareness that these spirits were operating through her and even seemed to be eager to cooperate with them.

As the week wore on, I lost some of my initial dread and terror and, incredibly, became almost accustomed to the situation. The occult student in me even began to enjoy the experience. I had numerous conversations with the spirits, questioning them and even answering them back.

Some of the personalities that emerged were characters that I recognized. A number of the demonic spirits spoke with American accents and claimed to be the spirits of the characters in the film *The Lost Boys*, the film that Jane had previously been so keen for me to watch. Another demon claimed to be the spirit of the lead singer of the rock/goth group The Cult. I asked Jane to explain how all this could happen and she told me that these people could project their spirits astrally into her and she into them.

The days blurred into each other as we focused on communicating with the demons appearing in Jane. We lost all sense of time and place. So it was a shock one day to hear an angry banging on the door. Jane was obviously troubled by this jerk back to reality. She told me to wait while she answered, and shut me into the room as she left it. There was some shouting on the doorstep and then she stomped into the room, picked up a pile of rented videos and took them to the woman at the door. After some muffled conversation, Jane eventually returned in a rage, cursing the woman, who was demanding payment of fines that had built up from the overdue videos and was threatening trouble if we didn't pay up soon. As we had no money to pay her, we decided to ignore the problem and hope that it would go away.

However, a couple of days later, when we finally ventured out to the local shops, we saw the woman from the video shop bearing down on us, angrily demanding that we pay her what we owed her, and renewing her threats of trouble if we didn't. We beat a hasty retreat to consider the problem, and Jane came up with a solution.

'Look, this electricity meter is full of fifty-pence pieces,' she said, pointing to the box on the wall of the kitchen. 'They'd never miss a few.'

'No, I can't!' I protested. 'I took a Star Wars figure from a shop when I was a kid and got caught. I decided then that pinching things was a dumb idea and I haven't done it since.'

'But Vince,' she said, in a persuasive voice that had a hard edge to it, 'you would be pleasing the spirits if you got hold of this money. They would see that you are obeying their instruction to look after me. Otherwise, we're going to be in big trouble for not paying the video shop. You don't want to displease the spirits, do you?'

'No . . . Of course not.'

Almost without knowing it, I found myself in front of the meter. Jane handed me a small hammer and I began work. After quite a struggle, I finally managed to gain entry into the box and a sea of fifty-pence pieces flooded out onto the floor. While I made a half-hearted attempt to hide the damage to the meter, Jane counted out the money. After this, we immediately went to the video shop round the corner and paid the woman. As Jane continued her argument with the woman in the shop, I let my gaze wander aimlessly over the assortment of brightly coloured videos, and was struck forcibly by how many were about demons, the occult or other evil practices. It seemed as if a malevolent force was everywhere.

10

Demonic Rage

On the day that her parents were due to return from holiday, a subtle and frightening change occurred in Jane. I had begun to think, almost complacently, that the worst was over, but I soon discovered how wrong I was.

A different spirit emerged on that day, persistent and sexual. Normally, she was reluctant to engage in any physical relationship, but now, under the control of this spirit, she became explicit and demanding, practically forcing herself on me and insisting on anal intercourse. I recoiled in disgust, unable to reconcile this perversity with our previous complete lack of physicality. I was certainly not sexually pure, but I could not go through with this act despite the demands, which continued for what seemed an age. The spirit, speaking through Jane, would not accept my refusal, unable to understand my repugnance. But I couldn't and wouldn't do it.

My categorical refusal to obey these commands provoked a completely new and alarming episode. I watched in total fear as a different personality emerged in Jane in such a way that it seemed to rise up from deep within her, displacing the previous immoral spirit. I had, to some degree, become accustomed to the various characters that spoke through her, but nothing could have prepared me for this new force that manifested itself at this point. She jumped up, screaming at the top of her voice, with white foam gushing out of her mouth. I have never before known such a feeling of absolute terror in all my life. Whatever was looking at me through her eyes was staring with the most intense hatred that I have ever seen and I was paralysed with fear to the very core of my being. My entire body froze and I felt my stomach contract as it was gripped by total panic. When I was able to snap myself out of my temporary paralysis, I snatched up a nearby crucifix – evidence of her parents' nominal Catholicism – and brandished it in front of her face. To my dismay, this classic method of defending myself had no effect whatsoever. Jane simply knocked it out of the way and lunged at me, swinging her fists and kicking out at me.

I tried in vain to protect myself with my arms as a shield, deciding against fighting back, as I realized that the *real* attacker couldn't be overcome in this way. During a brief pause in the beating, I grasped her by the arms, trying to reach the true Jane underneath the violent personality that had taken her over. Looking her right in the eyes, I cried out 'Jane! Jane! Snap out of it!' naively hoping that this might bring her back. But it was hopeless; the same evil face was still glaring at me with utter fury and hatred. Despite my best efforts to restrain her she easily broke away, shrieking abuse at me. Then, she ran through the rooms, hurling everything she could lay her hands on against the walls or onto the floor. She seemed intent on destroying all in her path; plates, plant pots, papers, ornaments, even furniture lay shattered and damaged throughout the house.

Something in me broke, and I lurched for the front door to make a run for it. But to my alarm, the door was locked. In a panic, I struggled to open it, knowing that I didn't have much time before Jane flew past in her destructive rage. Sure enough, she soon appeared and saw what I was trying to do. For a brief moment, Jane as I knew her was present, pleading with me not to leave her. I told her that I had had enough and needed to get out. Then, in an instant, the violent personality took over again and the same evil face appeared once more. More threats and abuse followed and when I realized that I couldn't get the door open I gave up and sank trembling on the stairs.

When she had exhausted the possibilities of destruction, Jane's behaviour changed again, taking on an almost eerie dimension. She began running into cupboards and giggling like a little girl. In and out of each room she went, climbing into cupboards and wardrobes, her manic laughter sending shivers down my spine. By this stage I was so distraught that I thought I was going to have a complete nervous breakdown. I was losing my grip on reality and couldn't believe that all this was actually happening.

Gradually, though, I became aware that Jane was calmer; a more relaxed personality had gained dominance over her. A familiar American voice spoke, advising me to clean up the house before her parents came back, which, it predicted, would be within just a few minutes. I scurried round, frantically trying to clean and tidy up, but to no avail. Within a very short space of time, the car rolled up and Jane's parents came in. Their warm, holiday-refreshed greetings turned to looks of horror and fury as they slowly took in the devastation around them. I stood in shamefaced silence as they disbelievingly surveyed the mess. I longed to justify myself, to explain what had been happening, but I could not speak. I could see that they were deeply hurt and disappointed in me. They had trusted me and left me in charge of their house and their daughter. I felt as though I had betrayed them. I was so shocked by the whole experience that I could not even begin to explain what had happened, and they turned their anger on me, maybe because they dare not upset Jane.

Jane though, had no pangs of conscience. She went into the other room to talk to her parents and I heard her telling them about me breaking into their electricity meter. When they confronted me, I admitted it with downcast eyes, unable to face up to their looks of disappointment and disgust. Abruptly, Jane's father left the room to phone the police. After an uncomfortably long time, a large, red-faced policeman arrived and asked me if I had taken the money. When I confessed that I had, I was taken to the local police station in Hoylake.

Jane insisted on coming to the police station with me. I yearned to tell the police what was really happening, but was sure that they would never believe me. As I was separated from her and led away for fingerprinting and photographs, she whispered fiercely in my ear, 'Don't you *dare* tell anyone what has really been going on!'

When I finally returned to the reception area, Jane was talking to two officers who eyed me suspiciously. It was obvious that they had been discussing me, and further that they had formed a very negative view of me. The officers looked me up and down as though I were the devil himself! Ignoring me completely, they turned to Jane and asked, 'Would you like us to give you a lift somewhere, love?' In her sweetest voice she replied, 'Yes, please could you take me to my parents' home.' Glad to be of service to such a pretty girl, they sauntered towards the exit, beckoning Jane to follow them. With a glare, she nodded at me to follow her. 'Where do you think you're going?' snapped one of the policemen. Before I could answer, Jane quickly jumped in, saying, 'Oh it's all right. I want him to come too.' They looked at her aghast and said, 'Are you sure?' She gave a brave nod and smile and they didn't argue.

Throughout the journey, the policemen constantly reassured Jane that she could contact them at any time should she need them. From my seat, I could see the driver's narrowed, penetrating eyes staring at me through the rear view mirror. I wanted to cry out, 'Why are you treating me like this? Don't you realize that I am the innocent one here? That *I* am the one who is being abused?' But I knew they had already made their minds up about me. Jane had put on such a first-class performance that my imagined speech would have been utterly pointless.

Understandably, we did not receive a welcome when we arrived back at Jane's house, but, to my great surprise, her parents eventually calmed down and allowed us to stay there. Of course, my relationship with them could never be the same, which made me very sorry.

To make things worse, Jane kept implying that *I* was the one who had led *her* astray! She reminded them again and again of my interest in the occult, tormenting them with talk of 'my evil occult powers'. I longed to escape, to return to my parents, as *her* parents encouraged me to do, but I felt trapped by fear and hopelessness. The words of one of the many spirits with whom I had spoken during the previous week rang loud in my mind, 'Don't even bother telling anyone what is really going on. After all, who would believe such a story? People will think you are crazy!'

11

Mind Games and Power

The following days blurred together in a surreal collage of aimless wandering, hot, humid weather and appearance after appearance of spirits, bombarding me with twisted facts and suggestions. It was as if I was in the grip of a nightmare, unable to wake up, unable to distinguish reality from fantasy, unable to get on with 'normal' life.

Jane co-operated with the spirits within her to devise bizarre mind games, all of which, I came to realize, were designed to break me down emotionally and mentally. One day, she pulled me into the local pet shop. Mystified, I watched as she headed for the mice, pointing some out to the shop assistant.

'Do you think this is a good idea? Your parents will hardly have us in the house. I don't think they will be too happy with having mice around too,' I ventured timidly.

Jane smiled her secret smile and ignored me, paying for the mice and thrusting the cardboard box at me to carry.

'These mice are very special,' she informed me as we left the shop. 'They will stay with us, because they represent four souls; you, me, Kiefer Sutherland [actor in *The Lost*

Boys] and Ian Asbury [front man in the band The Cult].' I stared at her in bewilderment, unaware that in ancient occult folklore, mice were often viewed as symbols for the human soul. As we had no cage for the animals, Jane insisted that I carry them around in the large cardboard box, which of course, was very messy and awkward; all part of the process of humiliating and subduing me. The box quickly became damp with urine and it must have given off a terrible stink. (As I have no sense of smell, I was fortunately unaffected by this!) In the end, we resorted to keeping them behind the nearby railway station, visiting them every day to feed them. To my relief, it was not long before they all escaped.

Jane used anything she could to frighten and manipulate me. She pounced on a tabloid headline, 'Agent of Satan!', and thrust the paper at me to read. Beneath the banner was a photograph of a man in his thirties, with a pale face, dark sunken eyes, and jet black tightly slicked-back hair, revealing a pointed hairline. He looked very much like most people's image of a stereotypical vampire. This man was a self-proclaimed representative of Satan, visiting the UK from abroad on a mission for his master. I am sure that the majority of readers would have simply dismissed this individual as a joke. Indeed, from the little I read, the newspaper itself didn't seem to be taking the story seriously. However, the article terrified me. I was so weakened in mind and body that I believed anything was possible. Panic-stricken thoughts raced through my mind; 'What is this all about? Maybe this person is involved in what is happening to me in some way? What if this person is coming to get me?'

My fears must have shown on my face. Jane, who had been carefully watching my reactions as I read the article, gave a smile of satisfaction as I looked up from the paper to meet her gaze. From that time on, she used the article as yet another weapon. If I so much as hesitated to obey her, she threatened, 'If you don't do as I am asking, then that person you read about in the newspaper, the one working for *Satan*, will come for you.' I believed her.

Jane encouraged my growing paranoia by appearing to know everyone we encountered on the streets. She told me that there were two types of people; those who were 'on our side', and those who were against us. As we walked around the town, Jane approached various strangers who evidently knew her quite well.

One man asked pointedly, almost as if he was talking in code, 'How is *the work* going on, Jane?' She replied meaningfully that things were going as they should, and then they both stared at me long and hard for an uncomfortably long time. She explained that this man was on our side. He walked off without another word and I was left feeling that no one was as they first appeared to be. Furthermore, it seemed that everyone had the potential to be some sort of an enemy.

In other attempts to break me down and to consolidate her control, Jane seemed keen on setting me a variety of tests. Her favourite was to force me to stare at the local gangs milling round the town centre. They were, she insisted, our enemies. Bitter personal experience had shown me that they were not very friendly. Moreton could be a violent place and local gangs didn't take kindly to strangers trespassing on their turf at the best of times. A few years earlier, some friends and I had been beaten up by a gang in this area. Yet here we were, two strange Goths, standing across the road from them and glaring. Jane stayed behind me, urging me, 'Don't look away from them. Keep staring! That's the only way they can be dealt with!' Most of the gang looked puzzled rather than annoyed. I kept it up for as long as I could possibly endure before the discomfort became too much and I gave in to my natural inclination to turn away. Jane was furious with me, telling me that I should have kept staring them out. It's amazing that I was not beaten to a pulp by such gangs. The whole process was set up to provoke such a reaction. Much to Jane's frustration though, her tactic never seemed to create the desired result.

I lived each day in a state of fear and anxiety. Not only was I frightened of Jane and her power over me, but also of the increasing number of supernatural phenomena which occurred. One night, Jane and I were waiting outside her parents' house, hoping to be allowed in early to sleep. Suddenly, Jane looked up into the branches of some nearby trees with an expression of horror. In a terrified voice she screamed, 'There is something evil in that tree that wants to hurt us!' Simultaneously, I heard a blood-curdling, heart-stopping sound coming from the trees. No words could ever adequately describe what I heard. It could have come from the pit of Hell itself. We ran and as I glanced back I could see clearly enough into the tree to observe that no one was hiding up there making the noise. I also caught a glimpse of Jane's expression as she gloated over my terror.

On another occasion, I was transfixed by faint and ghostly lights near the window of Jane's bedroom, moving very slowly and pulsating subtly in and out of brightness. I was totally amazed, having never seen anything quite like this, and finding no explanation for these flashing orbs of light when I rushed to look outside. In contrast, Jane showed no surprise whatsoever. She just smiled in satisfaction and yet again was more interested in watching my reaction than in the event itself.

'Do you see that man walking behind us?' Jane asked a few days later, as we wandered yet again through the town. I stole a quick backward glance and saw a middle-aged, scruffy sort of man, walking behind us. 'He is against us,' she warned. 'He is our enemy. I'll try and get rid of him.'

She lifted her arm discreetly in front of her and revolved her finger. To my amazement, the man stopped dead in his tracks in the middle of the street, did an about-turn, and walked in the opposite direction! There was no way that this man could have seen Jane's action, as he was too far away. And it seemed impossible that the incident could have been staged in some way beforehand.

A further example of supernatural activity came from a surprising source. I turned as usual to the horoscope page of the newspaper, while I drank my tea in the garden of Jane's house. Her parents had not wanted us to come in, but had relented sufficiently to dispense tea and newspapers as long as we remained outside. The words leapt out of the page, shocking in their accuracy and relevance to my situation. The gist of the summary of my star sign was that I was having to submit to someone powerful and was unable to resist their control and influence. In a similar way Jane's horoscope was also remarkably applicable and spoke of dominating and being in full control of every situation and having the power to subdue whoever she wanted. I realized for the first time that horoscopes were connected with dark spiritual forces of evil.

Day after day, the power games continued, till I was reduced to that fearful submissive shadow, following obediently up the street after Jane, unable to make my own decisions or express my own opinion. Much of the time, I was in a daze, not thinking or feeling, just responding automatically to whatever was said or done to me. After my attempted escape in the street near her parents' house, Jane was even more watchful and even more controlling. I was indeed a puppet on a string, jerked this way and that by a cruel, calculating puppeteer.

12

Torment

'We're going to get our own place,' announced Jane one evening. I looked up dully, unable to raise interest or even dismay at this news. Jane was flushed, but whether with anger or excitement was difficult to say. I had heard her having words with her parents in the kitchen.

'Why? What's up?'

She shrugged. 'They've had enough, they say. But *I've* had enough of *them*, interfering and telling me how to live my life. Besides,' she gave her secret smile, 'we need a bit more privacy, you know, to do the things we want to.'

My stomach contracted at the thought of what she might mean, but I didn't dare ask. If Jane wanted to move, we would move.

Our new bedsit was in the popular local seaside resort of New Brighton. The landlord was a large, suntanned, jovial man, and despite our dark gothic image, he seemed to take quite a liking to us. The room he showed us consisted of a large double bed, an old Victorian-style dressing table and wardrobe and a few chairs. We had to share the bathroom and kitchen with the other occupants of the building. To our surprise, rather than take any money from us, he actually *gave* us some instead. He felt about in his pocket and eventually dug out his wallet and produced a ten pound note. Handing it to us he said, with a smile and a wink, 'Go on. Get yerselves a decent meal.' Obviously my pitiful condition had struck a chord of compassion in him.

Although the landlord seemed to be a nice man, both the bedsit and the area that we had moved into were very undesirable. A high proportion of the population seemed to be drug addicts. Many of the occupants of the house were seriously addicted to really hard drugs. One day, on returning to the bedsit from a wander around the seaside resort, we saw a group of people clearly in the process of taking some sort of illegal substances in the shared kitchen area. Our sudden appearance surprised them at first, but when they recognized us as fellow tenants, they just greeted us and carried on as though they were fixing a meal.

Some of the tenants did try to get to know us, but Jane foiled their attempts with a brusque, unsociable manner, keeping her distance – and mine – from any overtures of friendship. She didn't want anyone interrupting what was going on behind closed doors. There was one girl in particular who persisted in knocking at our door and who seemed determined to find out more about us. But Jane never invited her in, answering her efforts at conversation with short, abrupt replies, which clearly signalled that she was not welcome. Understandably, it wasn't long before she gave up trying.

A new, even more frightening phase of our relationship began. Previously, Jane had caused me great mental and emotional suffering with her mind control tactics. Now, however, she developed a desire for violence as she sought to break me in body as well as mind. Almost every day she attacked me physically, displaying a surprising strength. During one particularly violent afternoon, I was punched in the face, had my eye gouged with her finger, and was drenched in alcohol.

Another disturbing change was an increase in the number and nature of the evil spirits inhabiting Jane. They became more mocking and menacing and never seemed to stop tormenting me. Even at night the ordeal continued. Whereas in the past I had managed to get some escape in sleep, now these spirits continued their relentless assault against me throughout the night. Even when I went to the toilet, Jane wouldn't leave me alone. She insisted on coming with me and invading my privacy while I performed bodily functions, humiliating and frightening me when I was at my most vulnerable.

I had become a vacant shell, unable to think or speak for myself, and weighing only about seven-and-a-half stone. In contrast, while I deteriorated, Jane seemed to bloom and become ever stronger. Her control of me was complete and she revelled in it. Often, she ordered me to do things just for the sheer delight of exercising power.

'Look at the light bulb!' she would command. As if operated by a remote control device, my head would turn to look at it. Jane would laugh in mocking approval. 'Look at the fireplace!' she would continue, and obediently I would turn to look, no more able to choose than a robot. My mind was blank as I did whatever she commanded. Jane liked to play this game frequently.

I lost the will to go on and just wanted to die, to be free from this nightmare. I couldn't take the relentless torment any more. I was so controlled by fear and a force of evil that I could not escape, could not fight back, could not even ask for help.

The supernatural was closing in on me. There were more and more incidents of odd, unexplained phenomena. My pentagram ring, which I had so delighted in flaunting at the youth group, began to burn on my finger. At first it was a strange, tingling feeling, but as time went on it became more intense to the point where it was very painful. I mentioned it to Jane, who nodded and smiled in a knowing manner, as if in approval. She didn't show any surprise nor offer any explanation as to the meaning of this strange occurrence. I considered taking the ring off secretly, but then imagined her angry reaction when she noticed. I decided not to risk it, especially as she was becoming increasingly aggressive towards me.

We didn't go out much – maybe Jane felt her power was diminished in public – but on the few occasions when we did venture out, we merely wandered round the seaside resort, a couple of dark, silent souls with ghostly-pale, desolate faces. When we came across local gangs, Jane yet again insisted that I stand and stare at them. Puzzled groups of teenagers stared back at the two weird-looking characters across the road and muttered among themselves in bewilderment. To her frustration, however, and to my relief, we never got any harmful reactions from this unusual activity.

One night, though, Jane announced unexpectedly that we were going to go to my old gothic nightclub haunt,

Planet X. It was one of the last places on earth that I wanted to be, but as usual I submitted to her decision.

'You need to be very careful tonight, Vince,' she said, as we made our way to the club.

'Why?' I asked, immediately alarmed. 'What do you mean?'

She smiled slyly. 'Well, I can't say too much, but there are people there who aren't what they seem. And they could *harm* you. Seriously harm you.'

My heart was hammering in fear. 'How do you mean, harm me? People know me there; they're not going to have a go at me. I've not done anything against them!'

'Ah, but these aren't your mates. In fact, they're not really *human* at all.' She laughed at the expression of terror on my face. 'Don't worry, you should be OK if you stay close to me. They like me, you see, but you . . . well, they might want to make *use* of you.'

'What are they?' I whispered, barely able to speak with fear.

She stopped walking and leaned towards me, her face close to mine. 'Some of the Goths in the club are actually *vampires*!' she hissed. 'And I've heard that they are wanting to sacrifice tonight.' She gazed maliciously at me for a moment and then resumed walking, gesturing impatiently at me to follow. I was shaking with dread as I reluctantly plodded behind her. So conditioned to accepting everything she said, so vulnerable and worn down by recent experiences, I was unable to question the truth of what she told me. I was like an open door, letting anything and everything in. Reality and fantasy had become totally confused in my shadowy world.

I also felt humiliated by the way I looked and anticipated that the people in the club would sneer at me because of the deterioration in my appearance. The once proud Goth, so concerned with his appearance that he used to spend half a day in preparation to go to this nightclub, was now about to arrive bedraggled, stinking, bruised and beaten. People were bound to stare at me, pity me, or laugh at me. In a place so devoid of human warmth, I doubted if I would receive any sympathy, help or understanding.

When we arrived at the club these worries were confirmed. The entire night was a blur of fear, shame and confusion. Many people didn't recognize me at all, such was the difference in my appearance from the last time I was at the club. Strangers standing at the bar looked me up and down, curling their lips in disgust. Others gave me a wide berth, repelled by my filthy, tatty clothes and strong body odour.

Eventually an ex-girlfriend and her friends *did* recognize me. They were so shocked at my appearance that they could barely believe their eyes as they stood before me, mouths open. Shock soon turned into pity. They asked what had happened to me, but of course I couldn't tell them what had really been going on. Jane was standing close to me, pretending to join in with the girls' concern, telling them that I had been having a few problems but that she was looking after me. When they realized they couldn't get any information out of me, they made a hasty departure. I watched them join the throng of dancers on the dance floor.

As the dark gothic music pounded from the speakers, I noticed that the words of the song were all about death and evil. The people who danced to the hypnotic rhythm were all dressed in black with face make-up applied in such a way as to make them look pale and sinister. I knew that there were some among them who were involved in various aspects of the occult. I wanted to stand on a table and shout 'Look at me! This is what happens if you mess with the occult. Don't do it! Stay away!' But what was the point. No one would believe me. The whole club had taken on a threatening atmosphere. There was no light, no love and no hope. Darkness ruled.

I wandered around the club literally shaking with fear, more sensitive to the presence of evil than ever before. I peered anxiously at faces, half expecting some of the Goths who passed me to morph into fiendish vampire creatures, who would bare pointed teeth and lunge at me. Images from *The Lost Boys* kept coming to my mind, making it all the easier to believe that something horrific was about to happen.

My nervousness and scruffy appearance were drawing unnecessary attention, and it seemed as if everyone was staring at me or whispering about me in some corner of the club. I was bracing myself to be attacked. My thoughts became more and more panicky; 'Maybe everyone will suddenly change into vampires, rush at me and tear me limb from limb. I'm going to be ripped to shreds by a bloodthirsty mob of vampires.' Everyone seemed like a potential enemy and after the things I had already experienced, *anything* seemed possible. I no longer knew what was real anymore.

But the fears playing in my mind, put there deliberately by Jane, were not realized. The night passed without any big incidents and we caught the tunnel bus home, at around half-past two in the morning. As I stumbled up the aisle of the bus to get off, past people I had once known quite well, I heard mutters and whispers like, 'He stinks' and 'Look at the state of him.' I felt their eyes burning into me as I left the bus and walked into the night with Jane.

13

Intervention

On very rare occasions, Jane allowed me to visit my parents when we were running low on cash. Doubtless she hoped that my mother might give us some money or that there might be a giro cheque waiting for me.

The first time I saw my parents after our move to New Brighton was very emotional. We surprised them one day by turning up unexpectedly. Their faces were full of joy and relief at seeing me again. I had been away for so long that I think they feared that I would never return. My father asked me if I was back to stay now. 'We have kept your room tidy for you,' he said eagerly. 'Will you be staying tonight?'

'I can't, Dad,' I replied. 'There's things I need to do.'

'What like?' he probed suspiciously.

'Just things,' I replied half-heartedly and tried hard to avoid his penetrating gaze.

As I hugged my mother, I began sobbing. There was tremendous release in the tears and in the knowledge that I could still feel human emotions, even though they were those of great sadness and grief. As my mother and I wept uncontrollably, Jane watched us, a sinister smile of deep satisfaction on her face. And my father watched Jane.

Before the visit, she had given me a thorough briefing as to what I should say to my parents. She concocted a story, involving gangs of skinheads, to explain the bruises on my face; bruises actually inflicted by her. I could see that my parents were shocked and concerned at my condition. But despite this, I unfolded my carefully rehearsed story to them, closely monitored by Jane who sat nearby. My mother appeared to accept the explanations but I sensed that my father was suspicious. The awkward visit ended soon afterwards, leaving my parents to wonder when, or even if, they would see me again.

During my latest prolonged absence, driven by concern and worry, my father had searched my room, desperate to find a clue as to the huge change in me. Besides the relatively innocuous books and ornaments on my shelves, my father had also unearthed some of the more disturbing books and occult items that I had made a special point of keeping hidden.

Shocked and distressed by his discoveries, he turned to the only help he could think of. He went to a local Anglican minister, Barry Gauge, and told him all he knew. The minister listened carefully and promised that he and the church would pray for me and that, if and when the need arose, he was available to help. My father also started to pray; though he was not a Christian, he could not think of anything else to do but cry for help.

At around the same time, my brother, Kevin, visited a local drug dealer's house one night to buy some cannabis.

While he was there, the dealer's brother, who was a Christian, came into the room. Bravely, he urged Kev not to be involved with drugs and told him that he needed Jesus Christ in his life. Incredibly, after this unexpected sermon, Kev immediately accepted what was being said, prayed for forgiveness for all his wrong-doing and became a Christian. His life changed radically from that point. Like my father, Kev did not understand what was going on but knew that I was in trouble. As a result of his concerns, he and a group of other Christians from his local church (The Wirral Christian Centre) also began to pray for me. God had come in on the scene.

A few weeks later, Jane and I were on our way to the Planet X nightclub in Liverpool. I sat on the train exhausted and devoid of energy, my head resting against the window. As I gazed blankly out at the outside world, I felt like a caged and condemned animal going to the slaughter house. My mind was obsessed with the prospect of another shameful night at the club.

On the approach to Birkenhead North, my thoughts switched to my parents' house, so close to this train station and my heart filled with pain. I had so many happy memories of boarding trains here as a child for family outings to the beach and other exciting places. Feeling that time was fast running out for me, I was overwhelmed with an urgent desire to see them one last time. Mustering up all my energy and courage, I asked Jane if I could see my parents again before we went to the nightclub. To my amazement, since she had seemed so set on going there directly, she agreed, though somewhat begrudgingly. Emboldened by this small miracle, I made a hasty exit from the train, before she could change her mind. All the way along the street, Jane bombarded me with her usual reminders to keep quiet about our activities, accompanied by threats of what would happen if I disobeyed.

After a brief and very awkward conversation with my surprised parents, Jane and I went upstairs to my bedroom. Soon afterwards, I heard my father calling my name from the bottom of the stairs – a very familiar sound. Instinctively, I made my way towards his call, but then stopped short, expecting Jane to order me to stay with her. However, she was preoccupied with my music collection and took no notice of me. I heard my father calling me again and the urge to go to him was suddenly stronger than the fear that had been controlling me. Before I knew it, I found myself drifting out of the room and walking down the stairs. This was the first time I had been alone for a very long time.

Dad was waiting at the foot of the stairs and swiftly ushered me into the kitchen, shutting the door behind me.

'What's going on?' he demanded. 'How did you get into this state?'

Looking down to avoid eye contact I mumbled the usual prepared lines, 'I was beaten up by a gang of skinheads in New Brighton.'

He immediately challenged my story, then abruptly dumped a pile of occult books down on a chair saying, 'Explain them!' I was speechless.

'I know who is behind all of this!' Dad practically shouted, to my further shock. 'It's the devil isn't it? He's the one wrecking your life – and that girl is in league with him!' I reeled as if someone had hit me.

'Dad, you don't know what you are getting yourself into,' I croaked, barely able to speak.

'Look, son, don't worry about that. I'm going to get help. I've had enough of all this. The vicar says he will come and sort things. You go upstairs and keep her occupied while I go to the corner shop to phone.'

'But Dad . . .' I tried to protest, paralysed by fear, but he took no notice, shrugging on his jacket as he left through the back door.

My heart was pounding like a drum as I climbed slowly back up the stairs and I fretted that Jane would detect that something had happened. But to my astonishment, Jane seemed oblivious of time and people as she danced in front of a full-length mirror to some gothic music. I watched her and surged with dread and panic, longing to undo the conversation with my father, and somehow stop whatever was about to happen. But even as panic-stricken thoughts chased round my head, I glanced out of the window and saw that it was too late. We had some visitors.

My father was walking briskly down the path, accompanied by a group of three men (two in clerical dog collars) and a lady. Out of conditioned habit, I turned to Jane for direction and said in alarm, 'Jane! My dad is coming up with some people!' Immediately, she was on the alert, but there was no time for her to prepare herself, for suddenly the room was full of people.

'That's her! That's the devil woman!' shouted my father, shaking his finger at Jane.

'You go into the other room!' one of the dog collars said to me. 'You,' he said, pointing at Jane, 'stay here!' I scurried out of the room, quick to respond to the authority in his voice, and my parents came with me, equally quickly. Jane was left with the group of people from the church.

I was very, very afraid and could not believe that the people from the church would be any match for the evil that dwelt within Jane. Indeed, I doubted that God Himself was any match for her powers. I remembered clearly a demon who masqueraded as the Lord, telling me that God couldn't do anything for me because the demons were too strong for Him! At the time I believed this. What could even God possibly do in the face of such unrestrained evil?

But despite all these doubts, I sat down on my brother's bed, shivering with shock and terror, and prayed the only prayer I knew – the Lord's prayer. There was nothing else I could do, nowhere else I could turn. No one had asked me to pray; it was an instinctive reaction. Even though the words of my prayer were all muddled up, I looked up through the window into the sky and prayed with every fibre of my soul. 'God help me!' was the cry of my heart if not my lips. It was early evening and the sky outside was dark and cloudy, but at the very moment that I prayed, the black clouds parted and sunshine broke through. A perfect ray of sunlight burst into the room, filling it with light and warmth.

'Look! He's heard you!' exclaimed Dad, overcome with emotion. And for the first time, hope was born in me. God had surely heard me and was involved in my situation. The three of us wept with joy and relief, experiencing as we did so an almost tangible presence of goodness and love in the room. In stark contrast, the noise from the other room was horrific in the extreme. I could hear the tortured voices of those spirits who had tormented me for so long, as they experienced the same torment. The screams and howls were ear-piercing.

Very hesitantly, trembling with fear and dread, I edged towards my bedroom. Jane was standing up, her face contorted and flowing with tears. She was surrounded by the people from the church, some of whom were holding her or lightly touching her. Some appeared to be praying in foreign languages, while others prayed in English. One or two people addressed the demons directly, commanding them to leave in the name of Jesus Christ. When she caught sight of me, Jane shrieked, 'Vince, I can see faces in torment, burning!' I didn't know whether it was a threat or a plea for help.

'She must leave this place,' said Barry quietly. 'Let's take her to her parents' home for the time being at least.' There were murmurs of agreement from the rest of the group, but Jane stiffened in fury.

'No, no!' she screamed at the top of her voice. 'I'm not going. Not without Vince. You can't separate us. No! No! No!' Her screams reached a crescendo as the men moved closer to help her down the stairs. Barry and his team had not anticipated the power and violence of these thwarted demons. Jane struggled fiercely to free herself, fighting with a strength impossible in such a petite girl. It took nearly the whole group to hold on to her, at some risk to their own safety. All the while, a continuous stream of words poured from her mouth, frantically trying to persuade them to stop.

'The salvation!' she kept on shrieking. 'You don't understand what you are doing! You are wrecking everything!' As best they could, they ignored her and inched their way towards the stairs, while I looked on in alarm and anxiety.

Just as they reached the top, and were wrestling with Jane to get her to descend, my father suddenly appeared from below, brandishing a large chisel, his face bright red, his whole body shaking with rage. Glaring at Jane, with chisel held high in the air, he roared, 'I am going to kill you! I am going to drive this chisel into your heart!' The people from the church, while still holding on to Jane, tried to block him. 'Mr McCann! Mr McCann!' shouted Barry, 'We can't allow you to do this!' My father was so enraged that he threatened to punch anyone who stood in his way, and lunged towards the writhing body in the middle of the scrum. A couple of men attempted to restrain him physically and the group grappled together precariously at the top of the stairs. Things were getting totally out of control.

'Dad!' I screamed as loudly as my already emotionally exhausted and broken body could manage, 'Stop! Please! Dad, it's not the way!' My father looked at my pleading expression and must have seen in my face how much I wanted this terrible situation to end. He stood there motionless as the anger drained out of him, head down and arms hanging at his side, staring at the floor in total disbelief at what he had so nearly done. One of the men quickly but carefully took the chisel away from him. A tragedy had been narrowly averted; a tragedy which would have been a triumph for the evil forces at work in Jane.

Despite her close encounter with death, though, she continued to object violently to all attempts to remove her. The sea of bodies continued their struggle down the stairs, with Jane in the middle twisting and arching her back, like a young child having a furious tantrum, all the while screaming and shouting obscenities. Slowly, inexorably, they made their way outside as Jane was dragged towards the minister's car. She caught sight of me and made one last, enormous effort to escape, commanding me to help her. One of the church team restrained me from going forward, and I watched helplessly as Jane was bundled into the car.

Only then did we notice the large crowd of spectators gathered outside the house, attracted by the huge commotion. Neighbours, police and passers-by mingled in gaping wonder as the uproar continued. The police had obviously been summoned by concerned citizens and were not quite sure what to make of the odd scene before them – respectable clerics grappling with Goths, an apparent kidnap of a young girl, reports of demons and Satanic involvement. It was totally outside their normal experience and they held back, reluctant to intervene. Some of the people from the church group spoke to them and obviously reassured them, for they did nothing beyond ensuring that peace was restored to the astonished street.

As soon as Barry's car had disappeared, carrying Jane and a couple of the team, the crowd dispersed and we went shakily back into the house for the traditional cup of tea to treat our shock. Two people from the church stayed with me to offer prayer and comfort. Now that the crisis was over, they were able to take in their surroundings a little more and were visibly shocked by the occult paraphernalia in my room. They urged me to get rid of all these things and offered to take them away and burn them. I gladly agreed to their suggestion and we filled three large bin bags full of books, magazines, models, posters, ornaments and candles.

Even though Jane was no longer physically present, I was still extremely fearful. She had made so many terrifying and convincing threats towards me and my family; threats I had believed, knowing the evil power at her command. Now that everything had been exposed, I was very edgy and agitated, imagining that something terrible was suddenly going to occur. I tried my best to explain to my parents how I felt and they listened to me patiently as I told them about the demons, the intimidation, and the supernatural displays of power I had witnessed. But they were out of their depth, unable to grasp the horrible reality of what I was telling them. They wanted so much to help me, but they didn't really know how.

That night I slept on the sofa in the front living room with my faithful father watching over me. He knew that I was still absolutely terrified that something awful was going to happen. I lay awake for a long time, eyes wide open in panic, imagining all sorts of horrific things happening to my parents and Kev, and then being left totally alone in the house; the last victim, waiting to share the same fate. Exhaustion and the comfort of silence eventually got the better of me and I nodded off to sleep, awaking the next morning from the best night's sleep I had had for a long time. We had all survived the night.

14
Jesus Saves!

It was so strange to wake up on my own, to go to the
bathroom without being followed, to make my own
decisions, to be free of Jane's controlling presence.
Slowly, very slowly I began to adapt to the change, hardly
able to believe that it would last. It was Sunday and I
decided to go with Kevin to his church, the Wirral Christian
Centre. I needed to be somewhere where I felt safe, and
believed that church would be a sanctuary from any psychic
attacks that Jane might launch against me. The dreadful
experiences of the previous day had at least shown me that
the church had some sort of power in the face of demonic
forces.

En route to the service we called for Mick, the person
who had originally prayed with Kev to become a Christian.
When I first met him, I was immediately struck by the
goodness shining in his eyes, contrasting sharply with my
own, surely noticeable evil. Mick, though, showed no sign
of judging me. He was warm, friendly and accepting and I
felt almost happy as we set off together for the Wirral Christian Centre.

As we walked into the large, modern building, the service was already well under way. About four hundred people were standing, clapping and singing. Some were even dancing! Everyone looked happy to be there – a new concept to me, having experienced only boredom in other churches I had attended in the past. It was all unexpectedly lively and vibrant. As I found a seat, the words being sung sounded clearly and unmistakeably, reverberating in my mind:

> There's not a fetter that you cannot break, Lord,
> there's not a demon that can stand in your way, Lord,
> there's not a principality, power nor authority,
> that is not under the feet of our God. [1]

It was as if someone *knew* that I was coming and had written that song especially for me!

Although I had always believed in God, I was confused about what it meant to be a true Christian. I knew that I was no saint, but I felt – as many people do today – that I was generally a decent person. I had never murdered anyone, beaten up old women, or committed armed robbery. I therefore felt that I must be in with a good chance with God. I imagined him looking down on me and awarding me points when I did something good, and possibly taking them away when I was bad (though since He is a God of love, perhaps He would overlook these). Therefore, if there *was* a heaven, I reasoned, the positives should outweigh the negatives and those Pearly Gates should swing open for me when I died.

[1] 'Thank you Lord for the Victory'. Used by kind permission of Colin Orr.

As the service progressed, however, I began to get the uncomfortable feeling that I had got this whole God thing all wrong. People there seemed to know Him as a person, as if they had a relationship with Him. And it didn't seem to depend on how good or otherwise they were; it seemed to do with Jesus. They used lots of words I wasn't really familiar with, but the essence seemed to be that Jesus' death and coming to life afterwards made all the difference to how we could relate to God. After the service finished, I was introduced to one of the leaders in the church who explained how the Bible taught a very different scenario to my previous understanding of myself as a relatively decent person; that each one of us are sinners *by nature* and that even the smallest sin separates us from God. So if He *did* weigh our good points against our bad, the balance must always be weighted against us. Jesus was the only one who could right the balance so that we could be considered as 'righteous', because, as God's Son, He was perfect, yet chose to pay the ultimate penalty on our behalf, thus building a bridge back to God.

As I listened, a dawning realization grew that I was *indeed* a sinner. I realized that I had done some terrible things in the past and that my mind was full of evil thoughts. Shameful things that I had thought and done in secret also came to mind and I knew that God had seen me at my lowest.

I repeated a simple prayer to Jesus, thanking Him for what He had done, turning from all my wrong-doing and asking Him to be the Lord of my life. Never have I meant anything as much as I did that prayer. I opened my eyes and said, 'I feel as though I have found what I have been looking for all my life!' I suddenly realized that all the things I had been involved in, such as the occult, the music I listened to, my gothic image, Jane, had been a search in all the wrong places; a search that nearly led me to utter ruin. At that moment, I was overwhelmed by incredible, wonderful, inexpressible waves of love and peace. I was bathed in the radiance of love in its most pure form. There was no doubt about it. I *knew* I had been united with God for ever.

There was general rejoicing among Kevin and his friends as they heard of my decision. People kept coming up and giving me a hug or an enthusiastic pat on the back. I almost floated home, eager to tell my parents what I had done. They looked a little nonplussed, but were pleased for me. In their eyes, anything which made me happy had to be a good thing.

The following days were such a contrast to my previous lifestyle. I was able to feel happiness and peace for the first time in many years. More than that, I felt *clean*. It was a wonderful sensation after all the fear and filth I had been experiencing. I was no longer living a shadowy, unreal existence. I had a new vitality and security which pervaded my whole being. Undoubtedly, I was a different person.

Despite the joy of my new-found faith, and the definite change for the better that it seemed to be making in my life, I sensed that there were still some dark shadows hanging over me. I couldn't define anything specific, and found it impossible to explain my feelings to anyone else. Yet I couldn't shake off the impression that something evil was lurking around me, waiting for the moment to pounce.

I didn't really want to talk to anyone at either the Wirral Christian Centre or the Anglican church about this, as everyone was being so positive. I spent quite some time with the pastor, Paul Epton, at the Wirral Christian Centre, and also with Barry Gauge, who had been so instrumental in bringing about my release. These were good times of follow-up to my decision to become a Christian, but the whole area of my involvement with the occult seemed skated over. The impression I got was that everything should be fine now that I was a Christian and my past was behind me. I really wanted to believe this.

On top of these feelings were anxieties left over from my past life. I was still very frightened that Jane would reappear in one way or another, or that somehow she would cause me, or others, harm. In the first few weeks and months, she did try to re-establish contact with me and kept writing long, manipulative letters. Every time I saw the envelope with her writing on, my stomach lurched and I was filled with dread. First, she worked on my sense of duty and protectiveness, telling me that I was 'in trouble' with the landlord in New Brighton who was 'going mad' because we owed him rent, and had left a disgusting mess on our hasty departure. She told me that he was threatening to call the police or come round to our houses and 'sort it out'. She begged me not to leave her to deal with it on her own.

When I failed to respond to these letters, Jane tried another tactic; emotional blackmail. She declared that she 'loved me' (something she had never said before), and that she was sorry for what had happened but that she had never had any control over the powers that exerted such a hold on her. She claimed to be free of the spirits that had tormented her and said she just wanted me back to start a fresh relationship.

The letters were a horrible reminder of all that I was

escaping from. I didn't believe the lies and deceit in them, but nonetheless I got so upset and angry when I read them that in the end, I threw them away unopened. Somehow, I managed to be strong enough to resist the urge to write back to her. After a while, to my relief, the letters ceased.

She never came back to the house – something I feared for a long time – but I did bump into her a couple of times at the station, getting on or off a train. The sight of her brought back all my fear and vulnerability; I was only a young Christian and found it hard to overcome these emotions. Strangely, though, on the few occasions that I did see her, she actually seemed more scared of me. She would smile nervously and then scuttle off, obviously reluctant to talk or really acknowledge me. Each time I saw her, she was with a large, blond young man wearing jeans and a biker's jacket. He seemed unduly nervous as well and I wondered what crazy thoughts she had been putting into his head. These fleeting encounters were the last times I ever saw Jane and, other than rumour and hearsay, I don't know what became of her. All I could do was to pray for her occasionally and leave her in God's hands. It was time to move on to the new life God had set before me.

Another big worry in those early days after I became a Christian was the nagging thought of my impending court appearance regarding the meter theft. The idea of standing in a courtroom scared me a lot and I was extremely worried about the possible outcome.

My first priority was to change my solicitors, as they had been insisted on by Jane, and I therefore distrusted them. I didn't know her motive for choosing them and I preferred to have someone independent. It was only after I had, with much trepidation, 'sacked' them that I noticed that they had an unusual name – Balaam, name of a controversial Old Testament character who cursed Israel and who is considered by many as an enemy of God and a practitioner of the occult. When I discovered this, I was even more glad to be rid of them!

The fateful day of the court appearance eventually came and I arrived at Birkenhead court very early in the morning. After a lot of waiting around, I met with my solicitor in a small side room. As soon as I saw him, I blurted out my overriding anxiety, 'You don't think I will go to prison do you?' He looked at me doubtfully, sighed a heavy sigh, and replied, 'I will do my best.'

After this I went into a cubicle in a toilet and prayed with all my heart that I wouldn't go to prison. When I emerged, I saw my solicitor chatting and laughing with a group of other official-looking people. They glanced meaningfully over at me and there was more laughter. I felt as if I was possibly the butt of some sort of 'in-house' joke though I wasn't quite sure what.

When I eventually appeared before the court, everyone seemed to have slight smiles on their faces and were looking at each other as though they knew something that I did not. The whole event was a bit of a haze as I was so terrified. As far as I can remember, I was to be bound over, ordered to pay back the money that had been taken plus a small fine. After receiving a stern telling off, I walked out from that court enormously relieved and grateful. Maybe at last I could turn my back on my troubling past and look forward to a far better future.

15

Poison Arrows

However, the evil forces I had dallied with for so many years were not going to give me up without a fight. I had been rescued from a monster whose tentacles reached into every part of me and that monster was violent and dangerous in its death throes.

I had experienced an amazing peace when I became a Christian, but gradually it leaked away, forced out by an inexplicable anxiety. Every time I attempted to communicate with God, perhaps in prayer or reading the Bible, this anxiety grew worse. I could feel it building up inside me, like lava in a volcano.

One evening, when I was alone in my room, the volcano erupted. I began to feel great turmoil and churning from deep within me. For a short while, I thought it was the beginnings of a virulent stomach upset, but then a great groaning sound came from that area and my body erupted in spasms and twitches. I crouched on the bed, shocked and frightened, with no idea what was wrong with me. I staggered downstairs, hoping to distract myself with some television, but to my dismay, as I sat downstairs, I continued to feel twitches all over my body and kept hearing the strange groaning noise coming from deep within me. I had enough experience of demonic attack to know that this was not a physical illness. At the same time, what can only be described as a black cloud descended on me and I sank into the deepest, darkest depression I had ever known.

I began to see horrific visions, heard tormenting voices and felt constantly troubled and disturbed. Once, when I had just closed my eyes, I saw a clear image of a darkened room with a mass of naked bodies all writhing on top of each other. I was so shocked that I sat bolt upright. The image was too quick and too clear to be a dream. Even when I was with other people, even when I was at church meetings, I could be affected by these disturbing visions or voices.

I found it impossible to believe what I heard about God and His goodness; it was as if there was a huge blockage in my mind which prevented me understanding. I began to believe instead that I had somehow done something against God and was being punished by Him. As I looked for answers as to why all this was happening, I thought that maybe I had failed some sort of test that God had set me and been given over to the powers of darkness once more. Perhaps I was finally going mad.

Some of Jane's words, reported to me by her aunt, haunted me; that 'the thing' (whatever that was!) connected to me would follow me and eventually destroy me. 'Maybe this was what she meant,' I panicked. 'Maybe my attempt to escape and live a new Christian life has all been in vain. Maybe these dark forces *are* stronger than God after all, as I originally thought. Or maybe God is letting these demons loose on me to teach me a lesson.' All of these thoughts swirled around my confused mind, tormenting me even further.

Desperate for help, I approached many people in the church, but though they were concerned and caring, listening to me for hours at a time, nobody really seemed to understand; in fact, some people seemed afraid of the things I was talking about. Receiving no significant answers or solutions to my situation, I began to feel very isolated and hopeless. I tried to pray, looking to God for a way out of the madness that had swamped me, but He seemed like a distant memory. And worse, the times of prayer themselves became a terrifying battleground.

Many times, as I bowed my head and closed my eyes, allowing my spirit to be open to God, I felt a terrible gripping pain in my head, just as if a claw or a bony hand was squeezing it. At the same time, the most hideous, nauseating smell assailed me. I retched and spluttered, nearly vomiting because it was so bad – and I normally do not have a sense of smell at all. The intense pain was over in a few seconds, but the smell lingered for ages. This same putrid stench followed me around, sometimes evident, sometimes not. It smelt like death, overwhelming and very distressing. Yet no one else noticed it at all.

One morning, I woke with a huge weight pressing down on my chest. There was nothing physically there, but I could hardly breathe because of the pressure. I jerked my body and felt something release from me. Immediately, there was the sound of running across the walls of the bedroom. I looked wildly around, but could see nothing. All I could hear were loud scuttling and squawking noises moving round the room. It was not a nightmare – I was fully conscious and leapt out of bed and out of the room as quickly as possible.

Everything which had previously been a support and a source of life and hope was being distorted into a threat. The Bible was suddenly full of condemnation, curses and punishment. Every time I looked in it, I read something (out of context, but I didn't consider that) which seemed to be aimed accusingly at me. Once, in a state of confusion and panic, I flicked through the Bible, longing to find some words of comfort and direction from God about what was happening in my life. My panic rose uncontrollably as I read (from Deuteronomy 28):

> The Lord will send on you curses, confusion and rebuke in everything you put your hand to, until you are destroyed and come to sudden ruin because of the evil you have done in forsaking him. The Lord will plague you with diseases until he has destroyed you from the land you are entering to possess. The Lord will strike you with wasting disease, with fever and inflammation, with scorching heat and drought, with blight and mildew, which will plague you until you perish . . . The Lord will cause you to be defeated before your enemies. You will come at them from one direction but flee from them in seven . . . The Lord will afflict you with madness, blindness and confusion of mind. At midday you will grope about like a blind man in the dark. You will be unsuccessful in everything you do; day after day you will be oppressed and robbed, with no one to rescue you.

I was totally convinced that this passage applied *personally* to me. For the next few days I waited in terror for all these things to happen to me, afraid to go to sleep, afraid to go out, afraid of the judgement of God, as I believed it to be. Needless to say nothing happened, and gradually I calmed down again.

Soon, though, *everything* seemed to be twisted and threatening; nothing was as it appeared and I saw cryptic, sinister meanings in all sorts of innocuous things. Pacing frantically around my room one morning, sick with fear and worry, I suddenly felt an urge to turn the radio on. It was playing 'Poison Arrows', by Mike Oldfield.[2] As I listened to the lyrics of the song, my heart froze:

> Somebody's out to get you!
> Hiding in shadows – poison arrows.
> Somebody's out to break you!
> Hiding in narrows – poison arrows.

An evil presence entered the room, paralysing me with fear. I was mesmerized by the words, perhaps unconsciously realizing the truth of the Bible's description of the devil's attacks as 'the flaming arrows of the evil one'. I was certain that the song was a sign that something terrible was going to happen to me and I was overwhelmed with dread and despair. When the song ended, I snapped out of the trance I had fallen into and the evil presence vanished.

But the attacks on my mind and sanity continued, isolating me still further and alienating me from those closest to me. One Saturday afternoon, when I was at a pub with some old friends, trying my best to forget my misery and be cheerful and sociable, I glanced down at my arm and shouted out in horror, jolting forward in my chair with the shock of what I saw. My left arm was covered in burns and

[2] © 1984 Virgin/EMI, from the album *Discovery*.

scabs, and the flesh was hanging off! I looked away in revulsion, nearly fainting, my eyes closed tightly and my teeth gritted. Bracing myself, I slowly opened my eyes again to examine the hideous sight, but when I looked again, my arm was perfectly normal. I gazed at it blankly, unable to take in what had just happened. Then I became uncomfortably aware of dozens of pairs of eyes on me. There was complete silence as all my friends stared at me as if I had gone mad. I couldn't blame them and, as the awkwardness of the situation became too much for me, I excused myself and got up to leave. My friends just looked at me and then at each other; the expressions on their faces spoke volumes.

Such strange behaviour became more and more frequent and my friends found it difficult to cope with me. Naturally enough, they could not understand what I was actually experiencing and felt that I should be able to 'pull myself together', 'snap out of it' and other such clichés.

It wasn't just my friends who seemed to be turning against me either. Even my father, who had been so supportive and a key person in helping me to get away from Jane, seemed to have lost all patience with my despondent, nervous behaviour. I sensed that he was becoming more and more irritated with me as he constantly urged me to 'get out and find a job or something'. He kept telling me to stop feeling sorry for myself and pull myself together. On the one occasion that I reminded him of some of the things I had been through, he reacted badly and told me that all that was behind me now and I needed to move on. He seemed keen to forget about the whole horrible episode and virtually deny that it had ever happened. I disagreed with him, saying that I needed to come to terms with it all and that my new faith as a Christian was helping me to make sense of everything. At the mention of my faith, Dad suddenly jumped up from his chair, his face red with anger and his eyes bulging, strode over to me and jabbed a finger in my face.

'You have got religious mania now! You have gone mad! Absolutely crazy!' he yelled.

'D..D..Dad,' I stammered, completely floored by this attack. 'It's not like that . . .'

But he didn't let me finish. 'First of all it's witchcraft and devil worship and all that claptrap. Now it's Jesus this and God that. What next, eh?'

'No, Dad,' I protested weakly, though I knew he wouldn't take any notice. My father's view on God was that He was there to help when we needed Him but we didn't have to get carried away with the whole 'religious thing'.

I, on the other hand, wanted desperately to become properly involved in the Christian life. People talked of their relationship with Jesus and I so wanted to develop mine. But it just wasn't happening. Every avenue to closer communication with God was being blocked or diverted. Even the church gatherings became times when evil tried to take over.

I was at a joint meeting once, arranged for all the local church youth groups. The speaker, a dynamic young man, introduced himself and began by telling jokes and strumming an acoustic guitar. He looked like the stereotype of a Christian, with a baggy T-shirt, sandals and long hair.

As I sat there, I felt an overwhelming hatred for this man rise up deep inside me. The feelings seemed to engulf me suddenly, and I had no control over what was happening.

Yet there was nothing wrong with this speaker (except maybe the sandals!). The problem was with me.

At that moment, Kev turned to me, laughing at a joke the speaker had just made. He stopped laughing when he saw my expression and said, 'You don't look too happy there, Vince. Are you OK?' I came out of my daydream with a jerk and nodded, glad to be rid of the consuming hatred. Later on, as we went home, Kev told me that I had been glaring at the speaker with intense loathing, with one side of my top lip curled up. I began to fear that even church services and group meetings would no longer be a safe haven from the enemy that pursued me.

16

The Battle Intensifies

And so it proved. The evil that had held me for so long continued to fight for me and used my new life as a weapon.

Things reached a climax one night in the house group when I was feeling particularly disturbed. I felt as though I was going to explode, the torment was so intense. I walked in and sat among the happy, smiling people, who were chatting and joking away with each other, and soon killed the light-hearted mood stone dead. When it came to my turn to talk about my prayer needs, I blurted out how terrible I felt and burst into floods of uncontrollable tears. Some people did try to comfort me, but had no way of understanding the anguish I was going through. The group prayed for me but I could not be comforted. My head was swimming and I could feel an intense grinding sensation deep within. I was on the verge of losing control. The evening limped to a close, but all the former joy had vanished.

As Kev and I made our way home through the concrete jungle of the housing estate, we became aware of a vehicle driving very slowly alongside us.

'Can I have a quick word with you there, lads?' said a police officer, leaning out of his van window.

'Sure,' we responded. The van stopped and two policemen got out.

'Where have you been, and where are you going?' one of the officers enquired.

'To a Bible study,' my brother answered proudly. This was not a standard answer and the policemen eyed him with suspicion rather than respect.

'What's in the bag?' he asked us.

'Oh, have a look,' Kev said enthusiastically. 'It's our Bible.' He presented the bag with a somewhat triumphant expression.

The policeman looked puzzled, unsure as to what to say next. Meanwhile, the other officer had been fixing me with an uncomfortable stare. I shuffled nervously from foot to foot until finally he said to me, 'You know Jane, don't you?'

I gaped at him, so he continued, 'She's into black magic isn't she?'

I nodded speechlessly, feeling the familiar paranoia overtake me. It turned out that he was one of the police officers who came to my parents' house the night that Jane was taken away, and it was clear that the events had left a lasting impression on him. After chatting for a little, the police walked back into their vehicle and shouted, 'Bye lads!' For some unknown reason, I shouted 'Tonight!' in response, to the further bewilderment of the policemen. For the life of me, I couldn't think why I had said this. I felt totally embarrassed, and the chaotic confusion in my mind intensified. I spent the long walk home voicing all my fears, my paranoia about the police and telling Kev yet again how dreadful I felt.

By this time, my brother, who had displayed such patience and tried to do his best to be understanding, was worn down by it all. At a loss to know what to say or do, all he could suggest was that I try to calm down and get a good night's sleep. He looked completely drained by my relentless demands. I felt so sorry for causing him such trouble, yet I couldn't seem to help myself.

I took his advice and went straight up to bed. Strangely, though, I couldn't get to sleep. I felt almost euphoric, as if a kind of electricity was flowing through my entire body. The sensation grew in intensity and I began to feel very panicky. My mind and body were being taken over by an invisible force. It was terrifying; I couldn't escape nor did I have any control over what was happening to me.

I was being drawn towards a box of matches on a nearby table. 'Pick them up,' urged an unbidden thought. 'You're going to burn the house down.'

I stared at the matchbox. The desire to pick them up and use them was incredibly strong. In a moment, I jerked into awareness and, horrified at what had nearly happened, I snatched up the matches to throw them in the bin.

'If you do that, you will just get up in the middle of the night, get them out of the bin, and still use them to burn the house down!' The words were so strong that they were nearly audible.

I contemplated striking each match individually, to ensure that none could be used, but then noticed a half-drunk glass of water and quickly dropped the entire box into it. Trembling, I sank onto a chair, hoping against hope that the crisis was now over.

Suddenly, a deafening roar jolted me to my feet. It was

just outside my door; the thunderous, spine-chilling sound of an angry lion. My stomach seemed to go into my throat as I became rooted to the spot. Then there was silence. After a while, I relaxed sufficiently to venture outside my bedroom. Surely, someone else in the house must have heard the noise. I knew I hadn't imagined it. I cautiously walked across the small hall and into my brother's room.

'Kev, did you just hear that terrible noise?'

'What noise?' he asked, bemused.

'You must have heard it, it was so loud. Like a huge roar. It came from out here, somewhere.'

He stared blankly for a while and then comprehension dawned. 'Oh, do you mean *this* noise?' he asked, moving his bed briskly across the lino, with accompanying vibrations.

'I was just moving my bed. That's all. Are you OK, Vince? You look a bit rough.' I nodded and went back to bed, not wanting to burden him any more. It had sounded so much more than a bed moving. The devil – described in the Bible as 'like a roaring lion looking for someone to devour' – was playing tricks on me.

I tried to get some comfort and peace from reading the Bible and praying, but yet again, my enemy thwarted me, convincing me that God was against me and showing me condemnation in every word I read. But I had no one else I could turn to for help. Eventually, I switched off the light and just lay there, begging God for mercy and an end to the torment that seemed to be so relentless.

The darkness was frightening. Something was there, brooding over me, waiting. A mocking voice spoke in my head, as clear and audible as if someone was standing beside me. 'Ha, the son of man going to his death bed.'

I quickly sprang out of bed and turned the light back on. Terrified, I cried out to God and clutched my Bible for protection, flicking through it for words of comfort. Gradually my eyes became heavy and the last thing I read before I finally dropped off to sleep was a passage from the book of Job:

Why do you complain to him that he answers none of man's words?

For God does speak – now one way, now another – though man may not perceive it.

In a dream, in a vision of the night, when deep sleep falls on men,

As they slumber in their beds, he may speak in their ears and terrify them with warnings,

To turn man from wrongdoing and keep him from pride,

To preserve his soul from the pit, his life from perishing by the sword . . .

His soul draws near to the pit and his life to the messengers of death.

Yet if there is an angel on his side as a mediator, one out of a thousand,

To tell a man what is right for him, to be gracious to him and say,

'Spare him from going down to the pit; I have found a ransom for him' –

Then his flesh is renewed like a child's; it is restored as in the days of his youth.

He prays to God and finds favour with him; he sees God's face and shouts for joy;

He is restored by God to his righteous state. (Job 33:13–26)

A terrible scream tore through the silence of the night – angry, protesting, evil. Abruptly, I was wrenched from my doze, on the alert once more. It was as if something had been prevented from getting to me. I had been protected from danger, and the force against me did not like it. I remembered the words in Job, 'if there is an angel on his side' and a renewed sense of hope surged through me. God hadn't abandoned me after all. I fell at last into undisturbed sleep, comforted by the thought that God was on my side.

17

Deliverance Ministry

The 'prayer line' waited patiently for ministry at the end of an inspiring Wirral Christian Centre service. Church leaders and those with a gifting in healing were praying for individuals. The worship band was playing quietly in the background. There was an atmosphere of purpose and expectation.

'What would you like prayer for?' asked the well-spoken, slightly patronizing man as he moved in front of me.

'I've got a really bad headache,' I muttered. 'It just won't go away.' The man put his hand lightly on my head and asked God to take away the pain.

'There, accept your healing. You'll be fine,' the man said heartily. 'How do you feel now?'

'Awful,' I replied. There was no point in pretending. The man was taken aback and a little defensive.

'Now, brother,' he protested, 'you need to have more faith.' I felt even worse!

There was someone behind me, praying quietly and steadily. I glanced round quickly and saw that it was one of the assistant pastors of the church, a Nigerian man. As he prayed, I began to shake violently and fell to the floor (much to the surprise of the well-spoken man in front of me!). A voice shouted loudly, spewing out words of hatred and mockery. It wasn't my voice, yet it was coming from my mouth. I could feel two personalities at work inside me; my own and that of the spirit that had its grip on me and was presumably responsible for making my new life as a Christian so difficult. This spirit was mocking the pastor, Paul, who had come over to me and was taking authority in Jesus' name, laughing at him at the top of its voice. Somehow, I was able to feel its arrogance and contempt. When the pastor kept commanding the spirit to come out of me, I could feel its resentment. Eventually, the laughter stopped, followed by fury and frustration. My body, too, took on a life of its own, and slithered across the floor like a snake. But then, just as the rage was escalating and intensifying, it suddenly died away completely. It was finished. I had a definite feeling that whatever it was that had exerted such control over me had lost its power. I seemed to be myself again.

Whether the demons were actually 'in' me (the thorny question of whether a Christian can 'have a demon' or not) is a matter of theological debate. All I know for certain is that there were evil forces in my life that were making things unbearable for me. There are some who will contend that it is absolutely impossible for a believer to be possessed by a demon, whereas others in the Christian community are willing to admit that even Christians can be afflicted with demonic problems in one way or another.

I think a major stumbling block in the whole argument lies in the realm of definitions. Different people have very different interpretations for such words and phrases as 'possessed', 'have a demon', 'oppressed', 'dwell or inhabit' and so on. Speaking from my own experience, I can say two things for certain: first, I know without doubt that I met with Christ in a very real, powerful and personal way the night I put my trust in Him and turned from my sin. There is no denying that I was born of God at that point. Second, despite the reality of my conversion, there is also no question that I continued to be in the midst of an indisputable and extremely frightening spiritual battle. Whether the demons were actually inside me, taking over my mind and spirit, or whether they attacked from outside, thus affecting my mind and emotions, I do not know for certain. All I can say is that there was real demonic activity going on as I found myself in the middle of what seemed like a clash of two kingdoms. In fact, since that time, I have observed that many people who have been heavily involved in occult activities prior to becoming Christians go through very similar struggles and experiences.

Another approach to the debate is to consider the way that many Christians still struggle with various sins or habits, even though they have a new nature. Just because a person is born again does not mean that they automatically become perfect or problem-free. Many people have to deal with a lot of baggage that they may have had in their past lives. But as the Holy Spirit does His work of cleansing and healing, that person is transformed more and more into the person Christ always destined him or her to be.

I think many Christians run into difficulties in this whole area because of the word *possessed*. 'How can someone who has become *God's* possession also be possessed by a demon?'

is the logical question. When a person comes into a new and living relationship with Christ, and is born again by the indwelling Holy Spirit, they are the 'possession' of God and Him alone. Much of the confusion has come about because of the Greek word *daimonizomai* which in the King James Version of the Bible translates as 'possessed', implying that the person is in the *ownership* of the evil spirit. Used this way, of a believer, one possessed by the Holy Spirit, under His ownership, the word is most certainly inappropriate. A more accurate translation of the Greek word is 'demonized'. *Thayer's New Testament Greek Lexicon* defines this word as: 'To be under the power of a demon.' This could apply to the believer as well as to the non-believer.

Even though the theological disputes about this whole topic are important, they are not much help in the practical situation of an individual (Christian or otherwise) who is afflicted in some way by evil spirits. It does not do any good for a group of Christians to stand around pontificating about theology when someone is being ravaged by demons. Rather than get hung up on the *location* of the demon, Christians should be prepared to take authority, in the name of Jesus Christ, over evil spirits wherever they reveal themselves and whether the person is a Christian or not.

It is a hazardous ministry and not all are called to do it. There are some organizations and individuals who profess to work in this sphere of deliverance, who are questionable and unbalanced in their approach. Deliverance ministry can be a realm where some people get into all kinds of extremes and see demons in almost every person and situation. Great damage can be caused by some of these ministries, especially when they choose to diagnose a problem as 'demonic' when, in actual fact, there may be a more straightforward and less exotic explanation. Real balance and discernment is needed in this whole area and, thankfully, there are many gifted in this way. Harmful deliverance ministries can often be identified because they are involved in all sorts of unbiblical and extra-biblical practices.

When the pastor of the Wirral Christian Centre challenged the demons that had manifested themselves in the church that Sunday morning, he did it biblically; in the name of Jesus Christ. The Bible repeatedly tells us that demons are to be rebuked and cast out 'in the name of Jesus' (e.g. Mark 16:17; Luke 10:17; Acts 16:18). The reason for this is that demons have to submit to the lordship and authority of Jesus Christ, as He defeated them, and Satan, at the cross. Because of Christ's death on the cross, the forces of evil have been stripped of their power: 'And having disarmed the powers and authorities, he made a public spectacle of them, triumphing over them by the cross' (Colossians 2:15).

It must be stressed that although the name of Jesus is powerful against demonic spirits, it should not be used as some sort of magic incantation. In ancient times, a name was always intimately associated with the person. That is to say, the name was virtually equivalent to the person who bore it.

Although I have heard of the name of Jesus being used by non-Christians with some effect against evil spirits, this certainly carries some risk, as the name is being detached from the person of Jesus. The Bible gives us just such an example when people who did not know Jesus but had heard of his methods were attempting to cast out a demon.

The result was that, even though the demon recognized the name of Jesus, it evidently realized that the men were using the name fraudulently and gave them all a thorough beating (Acts 19:13–16).

Demons are not to be underestimated. I believe that they are far cleverer and much more powerful than any human being. The only way they can be truly dealt with effectively is by someone whose life is totally surrendered to the lordship of Jesus Christ.

Indeed, I and many others in the church that morning, had witnessed first hand the authority of the name of Jesus over the demonic realm. But while everyone rejoiced at the dramatic deliverance they had seen, I still felt that all was not right. Although there was no denying that something evil had been uprooted on that memorable morning, I suspected that we had only scratched the surface. The strange inner turmoil that had become so familiar was still ever present. I feared that even now I had a long and difficult journey ahead.

18
True Love

She was sitting in her parents' home, laughing at someone's joke – slim, long white-blonde hair, sparkling blue eyes, a beautiful smile and perfectly applied make-up. My first reaction, probably the same as any normal male's, was 'Wow. What a stunner!' But I quickly dismissed any ideas of romance, knowing that girls such as her were out of my league. She was Donna, sister of Janine, one of the girls in our crowd, newly returned from Cheltenham where, according to the girls, she had just broken up with her boyfriend. I was very attracted to her, but because of natural shyness and low self-esteem I didn't even try to become romantically involved with her.

Donna began to spend more and more time with the gang and even started coming along to the Wirral Christian Centre. At one service, to our great joy, she became a Christian. As she listened to the preaching, she believed what was being said and put her faith in Jesus. She felt as if everything seemed to 'click into place' in her life from this point.

One day a group of us were sitting in the newly opened Pyramids Shopping Centre, a huge glass structure in the centre of Birkenhead. As we were all chatting away, I looked up to see Donna gazing at me intently. Her shining eyes seemed to reach into my innermost being. I was totally knocked for six by that look and couldn't get her out of my mind for the rest of the day. My head was in a whirl, but it felt so good!

Later, back at the house, there was a lot of whispering and laughing. Eventually, I was approached conspiratorially by one of the girls and told that Donna really liked me and wanted to begin a relationship. I was over the moon with this news, stammering with enthusiasm as I said how much I would like that. I could hardly believe the rapid turn of events!

After some months of marvellous courtship, Donna and I were married on 10th November 1990, in the Wirral Christian Centre. My parents were delighted to see me settled at last after all the traumas of the past years. I had initially been nervous of telling them that we wanted to marry, but when I finally plucked up the courage to tell my father, it turned out that he already knew and was very pleased for us! It was a dream-like day, reflecting our joy and excitement at this wonderful new phase in our lives. We didn't have much money, so everything was done 'on a shoestring' and we couldn't afford a honeymoon, but we felt like king and queen for the day.

We spent our honeymoon at our new flat – a run-down bedsit where we had to share a toilet and bathroom with other tenants. I always found this quite embarrassing and longed for more privacy. The whole place was shabby. Our bedroom was freezing during that first winter as the window didn't close properly and the wind whistled through the gap. We complained to the landlord – a large, fat man with long, greasy hair – but he didn't seem to care about the condition of his property or the comfort of his tenants at all and never kept his promises to make some repairs. All he cared about was getting his rent on time.

Even though Donna and I were living in such conditions, and were dreadfully poor, we were extremely happy with the little that we had. As long as we had each other, everything else, even my continuing anxiety and depression, seemed to fade into the background. We were blissfully happy and, as far as we were concerned, we were the richest people on earth.

Yet despite my new-found happiness and purpose as a married man, I knew that I was still not totally free from all the problems that had plagued me in the past. I expected, and had every reason, to be living life to the full, but I was still suffering spiritually, mentally and emotionally. And of course, if I suffered, so did Donna. She was sympathetic, caring and patient, but she could not really understand the spiritual torment within me. I constantly grumbled about how terrible I was feeling, relying on her sympathy to help me through.

One day, though, as we sat in our kitchen with a cup of tea, Donna surprised me by responding sharply to my usual complaints: 'You know what you need to do? Pull yourself together and stop whinging!'

I was shocked. She softened a little, but looked determined to have her say. 'Look, I know you are suffering, and I know that many of your problems are not of your making. I really am trying to understand, and you know I care desperately. But you've got to play your part as well and try to be strong. You're talking yourself into a worse state all the time.' She had suddenly realized that she had been 'feeding' my problems with her caring attitude, instead of helping me to resolve them. I glowered at her. This was *not* what I wanted to hear. After all, I had been swimming in a comfortable sea of sympathy up till then!

My immediate response was to go into a full-blown sulk, and this, of course, created even more problems. The blissful honeymoon period we had enjoyed was well and truly over, replaced by endless bickering and an oppressive atmosphere. I feared our marriage was being seriously damaged, but wouldn't do anything about it. Yet Donna's words niggled me because, in my heart of hearts, I knew they were true. I decided to try to put them into action. This change to a more positive attitude was a turning point for me and contributed significantly towards my healing process.

It was indeed a slow, painful journey. There were days that were very black indeed. The intense, relentless ache would nag away at me, paralysing my emotions and swamping me in an ocean of the darkest despair. On days like that no amount of thinking positively seemed to help. I just wanted to withdraw from everyone. I used to go for long solitary walks, talking with God and pleading with Him to set me free. He alone really knew exactly what was going on inside me. But God seemed so far away. Sometimes, I doubted that He was even listening. There were moments when I thought I would never be free. No matter how hard I prayed, or tried to pick myself up, I just couldn't seem to escape from the dark cloud and the tormenting feelings that lurked deep inside me.

19

The Painful Road

One evening Donna and I, along with a group of our friends from the church, were all invited to an anniversary celebration at a local pub. Many of us hadn't been in a pub environment for a long time and the experience was somewhat of a novelty. Things began well that evening and everyone was in good spirits. Other people we met in the pub seemed friendly and there was a great atmosphere.

But when it was closing time, someone had the bright idea of going on to a nightclub. Not everyone thought this was a wise idea and quite a few went home, but a group of us set off for the local nightclub. As soon as I arrived, I felt awkward and uncomfortable. The place was a far cry from the laid back and friendly atmosphere of the pub we had just come from. The music was so loud that conversation was virtually impossible, and the increasing press of other clubbers was quite unpleasant.

As I watched Donna dancing with the other girls, and noticed the admiring glances she attracted, I began to feel violent jealousy rising up inside me. Before I could stop myself, I stood up and stormed out of the club in a rage, knocking glasses and drinks over as I went. As I made my way up the stairs and past the doormen, I could hear the girls shouting after me, 'Vince! Wait!' I refused to listen to them. The fury that had gripped me was so overwhelming that I felt strangely energized by it.

Outside, in the cool night air, I had the irresistible urge to run. I raced up the street and over a nearby wasteland, eventually grinding to a halt by a derelict building. I squatted down, gasping for breath, and saw Donna and the others toiling up towards me. She rushed right up and held me, concern written all over her face. I felt ashamed of my earlier jealousy, yet could not shake off the rage which still bubbled inside.

In the distance was the solitary figure of Kev, abandoned by the rest of us and with no idea where we had got to. Great love and affection for him welled up in me, but as it did, it was met by an opposing force; something ugly and evil. I screamed at the top of my voice, broke free from Donna, and flung myself to the floor, writhing around as if in agony, a white foam forming at my mouth. Some of the group held me down so that I would not hurt myself, but I had become so strong that they struggled to contain me. Along with this sudden surge in strength was the emergence of another voice speaking through me. I cursed, swore, and screamed the most horrible words at those who restrained me.

In the midst of all the tumult, the police arrived and, not really knowing how to deal with me, told the others that if I had not gone by the time they returned, they would have me sectioned. Frantically, the group made a huge effort to get some control of me and finally managed to carry me

away from the scene. Slowly, painfully, I returned to nor-
mality, and allowed Donna to help me home and into bed.

When I woke the following morning, I was deeply distressed by what had happened. My actions were like those
of a madman. Maybe I *was* mentally ill. Even the police had
thought so and had been going to section me. And what of
the deliverance I had received so recently at the church
service? The spirit which showed up the night before most
certainly had a grip on me. Why had it not been dealt with
at that time? I was upset, angry and very frightened.

I ranted on at Donna, who was also very shocked by the
night's events, pouring out my bitterness and fear onto her.
I hardly knew what I was saying, such was the force of my
emotion. During my angry outburst, I reproached people in
the church for not listening to me when I voiced fears that
something evil was still lurking near or even in me. As far
as everyone else was concerned, I was free. The memory of
everyone's apparent refusal to acknowledge that there was
still a problem made me resentful towards them. 'And after
this,' I sneered sarcastically, 'people prayed with me and
said I was now filled with the *so called* Holy Spirit!'

Horror-struck, I covered my mouth and gasped, 'Oh no!
I have blasphemed against the Holy Spirit!'

'God knows you never meant it. Don't worry. You
haven't blasphemed the Holy Spirit at all!' Donna comforted me, giving me a reassuring hug. I tried to believe her,
but I knew that the Bible spoke strongly about the sin of
'blaspheming' the Holy Spirit, and I couldn't help dwelling
on the whole subject. The certainty that I was utterly
doomed beyond all redemption dominated my thinking.
Words kept repeating in my mind; 'You've really done it

now Vince. No hope for you. Might as well give up and go back to your old life and dump all this Christianity stuff.'

I was haunted by the belief that I had committed the unforgivable sin, and consulted many leaders in the church during this time about their opinion of what this sin was. They all reassured me categorically that I had not committed it – though one leader told me off for worrying about it, pointing out that worry is a sin; I went into his office with one sin and left with two! – but somehow, I could not accept their word for it. Yet again, all that I valued most was being blighted by distortion

As we lived so close to the church building, our flat became a convenient place for young people to gather. Much of the time, I enjoyed the company but one evening, a few weeks after I believed I had blasphemed the Holy Spirit, I felt irritated and suffocated by the number of people we had round. Every room I went into was a mass of noise and laughter. All I wanted was a quiet corner to hide in, but instead, constant knocks on the front door meant even more people had arrived.

In the end I couldn't stand it any more and began asking people to leave, becoming more abrupt with each request, and ignoring our friends' and Donna's embarrassment. Many left straight away, but a few stragglers stayed behind to finish off their various discussions and cups of tea. As my annoyance grew more visible, through my scowls and raised voice, the stragglers finally seemed to get the message that they were no longer welcome. As Donna came up to me with a look of concern, violent rage exploded in me. My whole face became contorted and twisted and I reached out with a clawed hand to grab her face.

Terrified, she ran out of the flat, calling for help to the friends who had just left. Infuriated by the sight of them again, I stood among the small group in the living room and screamed at them at the top of my voice, 'Get out, get out, GET OUT!!'

With this, I fell to the floor and thrashed about in a frenzy, propelled by a force I could not control. There was a gas fire nearby and I was conscious enough to recognize that, whatever it was that had taken me over, was trying to push me into it. It took three strong young men (one of whom was a bodybuilder) to hold me down with extreme difficulty so that I wouldn't hurt myself. They finally managed to calm me and get me into bed.

Donna was so scared by my behaviour that she urged our visitors to stay with us until the next morning. Some of them agreed to this when they saw how distressed she was. She didn't feel safe and who could blame her?

By the next day, though, I was reluctant to face up to my situation. Someone had hurriedly made an appointment for me to go and see Paul Epton, the pastor, but despite the trauma of the previous night, I had somehow convinced myself that everything was OK and that I did not need any help.

I lay in bed arguing with Donna, insisting that I felt fine. As far as I was concerned, it would be a waste of time going to see Paul. Overpowering thoughts flooded my entire mind; a chorus of voices saying, 'Don't go to that appointment. There is nothing wrong with you. You will make a fool of yourself going there. Nothing will happen anyway. The minister thinks you are crazy. You are wasting his time as well as your own!'

Whether these were my own thoughts or whether they had been impressed upon me by the evil spirits that had shown themselves the night before I could not say. But whatever their source, I decided that I was *not* going to the appointment. Nothing was going to make me go. Donna had other ideas, though, and resisted my very stubborn attitude. She even had to dress me in order to encourage me to go, such was my reluctance!

Her persistence won the day and I was soon walking towards the Wirral Christian Centre arguing loudly and being quite obnoxious with Donna and a friend, Karl, who had stayed with us from the previous night. Still in antagonistic mood, I went into Paul's office, determined not to respond to anything he said. As he spoke, though, I became aware of a great churning and uneasiness rising up inside me. Paul began to pray and I felt strongly the presence of God in the room. It made me cry as I felt overwhelmed by God's love and care for me.

Suddenly, I sprang up from my seat, stood bolt upright, and screamed, 'Stop it! Stop it! Stop it!' At the same time, I lunged towards Pastor Paul, my hands twisted into a claw shape, clutching for his face. He stepped back and managed to dodge it. Again and again I flung myself at him but could not reach him. It was as if he had some sort of invisible shield around him. I collapsed on the floor, writhing and screaming at him, 'You are just a man!' Paul rebuked the evil spirit in the name of Jesus Christ. Immediately, there was a change and I was myself again. It seemed as though something had gone. Paul felt confident that whatever it was that had caused me such problems had finally been dealt with. He prayed for me again, and this time there were no violent reactions. Instead, there was a wonderful feeling of peace.

Paul's confidence was well-founded. Never again did I have to face such traumatic deliverance sessions. I had finally seen the last of the demons that had tormented me for so long. It was a significant step on the long, painfully slow road to healing and wholeness.

20

Free to Serve

'Those whom the Lord sets free are free indeed!' Gradually, I began to know the truth of these words for myself. Through reading,[3] talking to other Christians, thinking and praying, I came to a far more meaningful awareness of my relationship with Jesus and finally understood that I could *not* have committed the 'unforgivable sin' against the Holy Spirit. A huge burden lifted. I was indeed free at last, and with this freedom came a renewed desire to *do* something practical for God.

But what? I noticed that many people spoke about being 'called to a ministry', such as going into prisons to talk to prisoners about Christianity, or caring for the homeless, and they were all excellent undertakings. These same people were always keen to recruit me into their particular ministry or work. Yet nothing really inspired me and I continued to feel that there was *something* I should be doing, but could not decide exactly what.

---

[3] Particularly helpful was *The Holy Spirit* by Billy Graham. Please see Recommended Reading appendix for a fuller explanation.

Some months previously, during our Sunday evening youth group, a young man had read out a passage from the Bible:

> For though we live in the world, we do not wage war as the world does. The weapons we fight with are not the weapons of the world. On the contrary, they have divine power to demolish strongholds. We demolish arguments and every pretension that sets itself up against the knowledge of God, and we take captive every thought to make it obedient to Christ. And we will be ready to punish every act of disobedience, once your obedience is complete. (2 Corinthians 10:3–6)

Later, the young man came over to me and said, 'I felt as though the Lord was telling me that that passage was a word for you personally.' Surprised, I thanked him but inwardly doubted that this could be a special word from God for me.

However, that night, when I went home, I opened a book on spiritual warfare and there, at the very point I had reached, was the same passage that the person in the youth group had read out just a little while earlier. This time I paid more attention to it.

I was reminded forcibly of this incident when I came across a small booklet I had acquired and forgotten about. As I started leafing through it, I was instantly engrossed. It was a critique of the small religious group, the Jehovah's Witnesses, written by Harold J. Berry, full of fascinating information and ideas. It caused me to think much more about other religions, exploring their differences and similarities to Christianity, and looking at how Christians might approach them. A Christian friend gave me a book on Jehovah's Witnesses called *Awake to the Watchtower*, by Doug

Harris of Reachout Trust. This intensified my developing passion to understand the Witnesses and share my faith with them. I soon accumulated a large amount of the Jehovah's Witnesses' own literature and invited a number of local Witnesses to my home. We spent many an evening grappling over Bible doctrine as each party tried in earnest to convince the other of its respective beliefs.

Meanwhile, amazing changes were happening in another area of our lives. In the space of just over a year, we had the joy of two new babies; our wonderful sons, Nathaniel and Edward. As with any new parents, we found the whole experience a heady mixture of delight, anxiety, excitement and stress. I had never had much to do with young children up to this point, and now we were teeming with them! The house was always full, not only of our own babies, but other people's as well, as young mums came to visit, or leave their offspring for us to baby-sit. I was out of work for a good deal of this time and took the opportunity to become a 'hands-on' dad. It was an extremely happy if somewhat nerve-wracking phase.

Even with the demands of fatherhood, I managed to pursue my growing interest in theology and eventually enrolled in a small Bible college run by the Wirral Christian Centre. I had never been an academic person, but I found that because I was so interested in the subject, I put my heart and soul into the study and surprised myself by doing really quite well.

After this year long course, there was the opportunity to go on to further study at Elim Bible College (now called Regent's Theological College) in Nantwich. I applied for the degree course in theology and to my joy, I was accepted.

So in 1995, Donna and I, with three-year-old Nathaniel and two-year-old Edward, set off for Nantwich, where we moved into a large flat above a chemist in the town centre. It was quite a challenging adventure for me as I had never lived outside the Wirral before and was also a bit daunted by the intensity of the study ahead and the pressure of learning new skills. Money was short, but we were able to support ourselves to a certain extent when Donna got some evening work in a local chip shop. This soon led to me getting a job in the same place, peeling the potatoes in the morning and early evening. Nathaniel settled into a local nursery school, which Edward joined the following year. Despite the busy lifestyle, financial pressures, and many other unexpected hurdles along the way, I immersed myself in research, learnt a great deal from the lecturers, and enjoyed myself immensely.

By the last year of college, everyone's thoughts were turning to the future and I still wasn't sure what God wanted me to do when my time there was finished. Actually, it was something that I really didn't want to think about and so went into a sort of denial mentality on the subject. I would have been happy to spend the rest of my days as a permanent student at the college, had I been given the choice!

Many of the students were talking about applying to become ministers in Elim churches and, swept along by their enthusiasm, I convinced myself that this was also the correct course of action for me. I didn't really feel a definite calling to do this; it just seemed the logical conclusion to the last few years.

Then, just as we seemed to have the next stage of our

lives sorted out, disaster struck out of the blue. I woke up one morning with an irritation in my throat which worsened over the next week. Eventually, I could ignore it no longer and went to the doctor. Several weeks and two courses of antibiotics later, the throat was still deteriorating. When the doctor couldn't find any discernable reason for the condition, he diagnosed it as stress-related. By now, I could barely speak at all. I was devastated. Here I was, at the end of my degree course, trained by the college to teach and preach publicly, now unable even to hold a normal conversation.

The last few months of my course were frustrating and depressing in the extreme. Despite speech therapy, which helped a little, I was still unable to speak much, and any prolonged effort to do so left me exhausted and in pain. I avoided social gatherings and became quite isolated. And eventually, partly because a minister without a voice is not much use, and partly because I still had niggling doubts, I withdrew my application to become a minister, even though I had been accepted. I was dogged by a sense of failure and the feeling that the past four years had been a waste of time.

Nonetheless, Graduation Day in 1998 was a proud occasion. Who would have thought that someone from a rough part of Birkenhead, someone classed as 'non-academic', and nearly destroyed by occultism, would years later be standing on a platform receiving a degree in Christian ministry and theology? I could only put it down to God's miraculous work in my life. I also believed that God must have some sort of plan in all the difficulties of the last year.

After a few months of reflection and relaxation as a

family, Donna and I decided that we could best serve God back in Birkenhead rather than remaining in Nantwich, so we relocated and I did some voluntary work for a few months with our home church, the Wirral Christian Centre. But the problems with my throat were still so severe that I was unable to continue working there. It was a heartbreakingly discouraging time, when all of our hopes and dreams seemed to have vanished without trace.

However, I had learnt to trust God and not be beaten by circumstances, so instead of moping at home, as I felt like doing, I enrolled in a free local course to learn website design. Through this course, my website, Spotlight Ministries, was born and has been online ever since. The site began in 1998 with some articles I had written in college, and a shorter version of my story, but has since grown to be a vast source of information about theology, apologetics, religious groups and beliefs, world views, issues and ethics, for Christians and non-Christians alike. Through the site, I have had many emails from people all over the world who have had similar experiences to my own. It has provided hope and light for those who have been caught in great darkness.

The website made me realize that my time in Bible college had not been wasted at all. God simply had other plans for me than those I had made for myself. I came to realize that the college course helped to provide a strong foundation for the work of the website and the ministry that God has called me to do. If I had rushed headlong into busy church work, Spotlight Ministries might never have been born, and certainly would not have grown to its present extent. And even the public speaking training was not lost for, as my throat slowly improved, God provided me with some preaching and teaching invitations. From being physically unable to hold a conversation with my own family, I was now speaking regularly on the occult, new age movement, cults and other subjects, in churches, lectures, and on the radio and television. I was serving God, fulfilling His destiny for my life at last, and loving every moment.

21
The Battle Continues

The devil is still prowling this world like a lion, seeking those he can destroy. He is cunning in the devices he uses to deceive people and blinds them to the fact that God wants to rescue people and restore them. There are many 'poison arrows', as in the Mike Oldfield song, finding targets in the hearts and minds of men and women. Occult practices are becoming ever more prevalent and acceptable today. When I was involved in these activities in the late 1980s, it was still considered somewhat radical and unusual to be open in the practice of witchcraft and the occult. These days, however, many people, even schoolchildren, are becoming openly involved in it and unfortunately this is likely to be seen as more and more acceptable as time goes on.

I am convinced that there is a full-scale plan, put in place by the spiritual forces of evil under the command of Satan, to desensitize young people to all aspects of the occult by making the dark supernatural familiar, attractive and normal to them. Television programmes like *Buffy the Vampire Slayer, Charmed*, and even the *Harry Potter* films and books, provide a foundation for later interest in the real world of the occult. Although these fictional characters are in many ways far removed from the real world of occultism, there are some elements of actual occult practices intermingled with the fiction, and running alongside the special effects and fantasy creatures.

One popular and growing kind of witchcraft at the moment is the religion of 'Wicca'. There is much debate about the actual meaning of this term and some of its adherents contend that it is not witchcraft at all, whereas others argue that it is. The word itself derives from the old English word for witch. Although some followers of Wicca assert that the religion pre-dates Christianity, in actual fact it can only be traced back to the early 1950s as an identifiable religion. An Englishman called Gerald Gardner claimed that he had stumbled upon a secretive and ancient form of witchcraft, revealed to him by a witch called 'Old Dorothy' in 1939, in the New Forest, England. However, the evidence seems to suggest that he actually borrowed from a variety of different occult sources and put them together to make his own religion. Some of the many sources that Gardner took for his new religion include Freemasonry, Rosicrucianism, The Ordo Templi Orientis (OTO), ideas from the infamous black magician Aleister Crowley, and many other well known concepts and ideas from popular occult literature of Gardner's own time. Wicca has become the new, more acceptable face of witchcraft, dressed up in glossy pop culture packaging, and made more appealing to today's spiritually hungry world.

Wiccans and other modern witches often complain that they are misinterpreted by many Christians as being devil worshippers, stressing that they do not believe in the devil as a personal being. This is true, and Christians do need to understand the differences here. If Christians fail to understand what people in modern witchcraft actually believe, and misrepresent them, then they are unlikely to make much of an impression. Christians need to be careful to have at least a reasonable understanding of what others believe before they seek to communicate with them. This doesn't mean that every Christian has to become an expert on other religions before they can share their faith. It simply means that if we think we know something, we should be able to back up what we say. If we are uncertain about what a person believes, it is far better just to ask them first, before talking about Christian belief. This has the advantage of earning a listening ear for what we want to share with them.

However, just because someone denies the existence of the devil does not mean that he does not actually exist. It must be stressed that those who engage in occult practices, whether they believe in the existence of Satan or not, run the very high risk of *unknowingly* being in contact with demonic spirits, through their spells, magic and rituals.

The same can also be said for other modern forms of occultism, such as the New Age movement. This is an umbrella term that encompasses a wide variety of eastern and modern spiritualities. Like Wicca, it is another acceptable-looking forum in which to practise occultism, repackaged to look attractive to modern people in the West. Practices like meditation, yoga, reiki, channelling, and beliefs such as reincarnation, karma, the divinity of human beings are all designed to sweep people down a slippery, dark path, further and further away from the salvation that is to be found in Jesus Christ. Those involved in the New Age movement are constantly searching for the latest spiritual fad, hoping to unlock some secret, esoteric knowledge that will take them to a new and deeper level of spiritual enlightenment. Instead, the search continues and they are never truly satisfied or fulfilled. Indeed, most become increasingly self-obsessed, insecure and neurotic.

It should not surprise us that the poison arrows that Satan fires into society today should take an attractive form. The Bible tells us that Satan himself 'masquerades as an angel of light' (2 Corinthians 11:14). This is particularly seen in the popular practice of seeking to make contact with spirits through channelling and spiritualism. Many of the prominent voices in modern-day occultism advocate and encourage communication with spirits and other incorporeal entities, but the practices of spiritualism and channelling places a specific emphasis on making contact with them. On a scale not seen since ancient times, people are trying to contact numerous spirit beings such as angels, fairies, the dead, extra-terrestrials, or other beings. Although these spirits make high claims for themselves, and can certainly provide *some* information that is verifiable, their natural tendency is to lie and deceive. This is because, despite the many different masks that these entities wear, they are never what they really claim to be. Instead, as I found out so traumatically with Jane, they are actually lying demons, disguised as things they are not.

It is not extraordinary that evil spirits lie about who they are, since the king of all demons, Satan, is the supreme liar and master of deception. In the Bible, he is seen as the ruler of the demons (Mark 3:22; Matthew 12:24–26; Luke

11:15). As Satan is a liar (John 8:44), we can expect nothing but lies from the demons that serve him.

Many people who make themselves partners with such spirits have often found themselves becoming utterly tormented and enslaved by them. Again, the Bible speaks authoritatively on the subject. The devil is seen as the adversary of humanity, striving to crush people (1 Peter 5:8). His work is to steal, kill and destroy (John 10:10). He has taken humans captive to do his will (2 Timothy 2:26), he oppresses (Acts 10:38), and blinds them from the message of Christ (2 Corinthians 4:4). It is no coincidence, therefore, that those who have engaged in contact with demonic spirits (whatever they falsely claim to be) should often be so indifferent, or even openly opposed, to the message of the Bible. These spirits are expert manipulators and will subtly influence and bend the minds of people who are embroiled with them, usually without the victim even being aware of what is happening.

It is also no coincidence that at the same time that we are seeing a revival in the occult, we are also witnessing a subtle contempt for Christianity in general by society through the media – newspapers, magazines, music and television – and through much 'political correctness'. The devil is behind this undermining assault and most people do not even realize what is going on. Christians are perceived as weak, unfashionable and misguided and the church is portrayed as irrelevant, hypocritical, boring and dying. Those who reject this image of Christianity do not recognize that they have been very subtly misled into rejecting a false version that has very little similarity to the real thing. Real Christianity is life-changing, relevant, exciting, liberating and, most of all, is about coming into a wonderful relationship with God.

In fact, the only solution to the problem of occult power and demonic control is to come into right relationship with God through Jesus Christ. Satan knows that Christ defeated him on the cross (Colossians 2:15; 1 John 3:8), thus making the way open for humanity to come into relationship with God (1 Peter 2:24; 3:18). Not wanting people to find this new life, Satan does everything in his power to deceive and harden the hearts and minds of society against Christianity and force people into spiritual bondage through contact with the demons that obey his commands.

22
Hope for All

Maybe you are someone who feels the need to escape occult bondage and demonic control. If you have been involved in any of the practices briefly discussed in the previous chapter, or similar areas of occultism, you need to know that the pursuit of such activities and practices will never bring you true peace, fulfilment or security. In fact, as the story in this book has shown, it could wreck your life.

If you are looking for a way out, then Jesus Christ is the route to freedom. He said: 'I am the way and the truth and the life' (John 14:6). He is 'the way' because even though people in today's world pretend that they have got it all together, they are actually lost, scared and confused. People are secretly wondering what their lives are all about and are looking for direction. Jesus Christ provides that when we commit our lives to Him.

He is also 'the truth' because in today's spiritual supermarket of ideas, where every new philosophy and spiritual theory is jostling and competing for the public's attention, and telling us that truth is an individual thing, He is the voice who boldly declares to be the source of all truth and certainty. We are living in a world without conviction and absolutes, and even though society shouts that it is arrogant to declare that there is only one truth or one way, people actually do need and crave the stability of fixed reference points.

He is 'the life' because people are dead inside, ravaged by the hollow promises of the world with all its empty glitter. Although the wide range of spiritualities in today's world promise to fulfil and enlighten, many people are still left with that empty void nagging at them, which ultimately leads them into further experimentation. The final result, though, is not enlightenment but rather a spiritual dead-end of hopelessness and despair.

Maybe you have had similar experiences to those described in this book. You have been tormented, harassed and frightened by strange spiritual forces. These may manifest themselves as ghosts, or something else. Whatever way these spirits choose to come, and whatever mask they may be wearing, they are all evil spirits, under the control of Satan, intent on the spiritual ruin of humanity. If this is your experience, then please know that Jesus Christ is more than able to help you be free. John's Gospel says: 'So if the Son sets you free, you will be free indeed' (John 8:36). It is not God's will that you remain in a condition of fear, bondage, and submission to the whims and control of the devil's spirits. Jesus Christ came 'to destroy the devil's work' (1 John 3:8). Put your trust in Him. He will disperse the darkness and set you free. The prayer below will help in the first steps towards getting free.

Or maybe, after reading this story, you have difficulty

relating it to your own life in any meaningful way. Whatever your experience, I would like you to know that although my story is unusual, it illustrates something that is true for everyone, no matter what problem you may be going through, or what your background is. If you look to Jesus Christ, and put your trust in Him, He will not fail you. He is able to deliver you from *any* and *every* bad situation. Don't despair. Trust in *Him*, not religion, or a philosophy. These will fail you. Jesus Christ will not. The story you have read is actually very relevant to every human being, whether Christian or not, whether targeted directly by evil spiritual forces, as I was, or not. The message of Christ is for every person. It is a simple one, yet profoundly deep and powerful. Throughout the ages, it has stood the test of time and has changed the lives of millions. Christ is still setting people free from seemingly impossible situations today.

The central theme of the Bible is the Person of Jesus Christ, and the focus on His death and resurrection (e.g. Acts 2:22–24, 32, 36; 10:38–43). The Bible tells us that every human being is contaminated by this spiritual sickness called sin which separates us from God (Romans 3:23; 5:12). At the cross Jesus took our sin upon Himself and, in return, for those who will accept it, credits us with *His* righteousness in return (2 Corinthians 5:21). An early church leader, Athanasius, called this 'the amazing exchange'; our sin given up and swapped for His righteousness. This is the only way to be made right in the sight of God, not by any of our own good deeds as these can never be good enough, but rather depending fully on Christ and all He has done.

If you are not a Christian and want to make a new start with God, the Bible shows us how we can do this. It may be worth thinking over the references here and looking them up for yourself in a Bible.

First, you simply need to come to Jesus (Matthew 11:28; John 5:39–40, 6:35–37, 41–45, 65; 7:37-39). As people came to Jesus in times past, the way is still open for people to come to Him today, in prayer and in an attitude of faith, humility and repentance.

You need to come having belief in Him (John 3:15–16, 36; 5:24). Belief can also mean having trust in Him as well. If you believe in someone, you trust them. This is how we need to come to Christ.

As each one of us has done many wrong things, and our sin separates us from God (Romans 3:23), you need to be willing to turn away from the wrong-doing (sin) in your life (Mark 1:15; Acts 3:19). Also be assured that there is *no* sin so bad that God cannot forgive or that Christ's death on the cross did not pay for.

Finally, *receive* Jesus into your life (John 1:12; Revelation 3:20; Colossians 2:6). Ask Jesus to come into your life and to take charge of your circumstances, and be Lord of all you say, think and do. Promise Him that you will seek to serve Him from this day on. And receive His overwhelming, unconditional love and grace.

Some people find it useful to pray a prayer similar to the following. This is just a suggestion based upon the above Scripture references. But the formula is not important. If you are sincere, and really turn to Christ with all your heart, God will hear your prayer and freely give you His gift of salvation:

Lord Jesus Christ, I believe that you died for my sins and came alive again to give me a new life. I am sorry for the wrong things I

have done, said and thought. I know I have sinned. I ask you to for-
give me and come into my life to change me and give me a new start.
I receive you into my life now as Lord and will follow you from this
day on and always. In your name, Jesus. Amen.

If you sincerely prayed the prayer above, or one similar
to it, believe that God has heard that prayer and has saved
you. There need not have been a profound spiritual experience. Although the feelings I had when I became a Christian were unexpected and comforting, we should never base
our faith on feelings alone. The Bible clearly tells us that our
salvation is by simple repentance and faith in Christ, not
feelings. If feelings accompany our confession of faith, that's
great. If they do not, it is nothing to worry about. Feelings
come and go, whereas God's promises in His Word are
unshakeable and everlasting.

The next steps in your new Christian life are: get to know
Christ (Philippians 3:8; John 17:3), follow Him and obey
His teachings (John 12:26; Colossians 2:6), be baptized as a
declaration of your faith in the Lord (Acts 10:47–48).
Finally, pray and read God's Word regularly, and find a good
Bible-based church so that you can meet with other Chris-
tians and be encouraged and built up in your faith.

And *enjoy* your new life! It's the best decision you have
ever made.

I have travelled a long, hard road, with many obstacles
and setbacks. Yet I have always known that Christ was with
me through it all. When I think about the things that the
Lord has done for me, the hopeless and dark situations that
He has brought me out of, I remember again his words in
John's Gospel; 'So if the Son sets you free, you will be free
indeed.' In one sense, our freedom occurs immediately, at

the point of becoming a Christian. But in another sense, for some people, especially if their lives have been previously damaged in some way or other, as mine had been, the healing may be long and gradual. God, in his love and power, works it all for His own plan, purpose and timing.

Although my story is extraordinary and shocking, its underlying message holds true for everyone; that evil, whatever way it may manifest itself, is a tragic reality in our world, afflicting many people in terrible and destructive ways. But there is Someone who shines brightly like a light, has stood the test of time, and gives hope, peace and deliverance from evil to all. He is Jesus Christ and I conclude by letting Him have the final words to this book:

'I am the light of the world. Whoever follows me will never walk in darkness, but will have the light of life.' (John 8:12)

Recommended Reading

While these sources are recommended as useful resources, this does not mean that the author necessarily agrees with all contents.

The Occult

- *The Facts on Spirit Guides: How to Avoid the Seduction of the Spirit World and Demonic Powers,* John Ankerberg and John Weldon (Harvest House Publishers).
  Only a small booklet but not to be underestimated. Packed full of valuable information and well referenced.
- *The Siren Call of Hungry Ghosts: A Riveting Investigation into Channeling and Spirit Guides,* Joe Fisher (Paraview Press).
  In this book the reader follows British born author and journalist, Joe Fisher, as he investigates the whole phenomena of spiritualism, channelling and mediums. It should be noted at the outset that Fisher is not a Christian, and I only mention it here as it is interesting to see how some of his final conclusions reflect a Christian

world view. A riveting account and one of the most eye-opening and informative books I have ever read on this subject. Very highly recommended.

*   *Paganism and the Occult*, Kevin Logan (Kingsway Publications).
    A good all-round overview of the world of the occult and how Christians should respond.
*   *From Witchcraft to Christ*, Doreen Irvine (Kingsway Publications).
    The well known true life story of Doreen Irvine who became involved in 'queen of the witches' but eventually found freedom in Christ. A great personal encouragement to me in my early days as a Christian.
*   *From Darkness to Light*, Jeff Harshbarger (Bridge-Logos).
    Jeff was a Satanist prior to his conversion to Christ and this book explores his journey into the dark world of the occult and his eventual deliverance from it.

    The book is divided into three main parts with the main first section being Jeff's own story. The second part seeks to define what the occult actually is. The final part offers some practical advice and has a few brief accounts of others who have had similar stories.
*   *Witchcraft: Exploring the World of Wicca*, Craig S. Hawkins (Baker Books).
    An in-depth Christian examination of the modern world of witchcraft.

The New Age Movement

*   *Close Encounters with the New Age*, Kevin Logan (SP Trust).
    Follow vicar, Kevin Logan, as he travels to the New Age

mecca of the UK, Findhorn, Scotland, as he seeks to better understand society's growing fascination with alternative spiritualities. Absolutely fascinating and extremely informative.

- *Revealing the New Age Jesus*, Douglas Groothuis (Inter-Varsity Press).
An in-depth look at some of the false Christs of the New Age movement.

Deliverance/Exorcism

- *They Shall Expel Demons*, Derek Prince (DPM).
A very well-balanced and scripturally grounded book on a much needed, but sadly neglected and misunderstood, ministry in the church.

Cults/New Religious Movements

- *Awake to the Watchtower*, Doug Harris (Reachout Trust).
A book which was instrumental in opening my eyes to the opportunity that Christians have for reaching those in other religious movements. This book has recently just been republished and updated.
- *Reasoning from the Scriptures with the Jehovah's Witnesses*, Ron Rhodes (Harvest House Publishers).
Excellent book for Christians to reach out and better understand Jehovah's Witnesses. Good for scriptural discussions with the Witnesses. Well referenced and set out in a very easy to understand format.
- *Reasoning from the Scriptures with the Mormons*, Ron Rhodes and Marian Bodine (Harvest House Publishers).

As with the above, an excellent evangelistic reference tool for Christians to better reach out and witness to members of the Mormon Church. Good reference book for discussing biblical passages with the Mormons.

• *The Changing World of Mormonism*, Jerald Sandra Tanner (Moody Press).
Full of photo documentation and valuable information. A great resource in helping Christians to be better equipped to demonstrate some of the problems and difficulties apparent in Mormonism.

General

• *Christianity – a Ready Defence: Over 60 Vital Lines of Defence for Christianity*, Josh McDowell (Here's Life Publishers Inc.).
A useful reference book full of responses to common criticisms of Christianity.

• *Systematic Theology*, Wayne Grudem (Inter-Varsity Press).
A very thorough yet easy to understand systematic theology of Christian belief. Recommended to me by a Bible lecturer who said: 'If you only own one book on systematic theology let it be this one.' After reading it I had to agree. Covers every aspect of Christian doctrine and even goes into areas where other systematic theologies have not ventured. An excellent resource.

• *The Holy Spirit*, Billy Graham (Fount Paperbacks).
One of the first Christian books I ever read. The section on the meaning of the blasphemy of the Holy Spirit was of particular personal encouragement to me.

Useful Websites

The following websites were active at the time of going to publication:

- Website of Vince McCann, Spotlight Ministries: www.spotlightministries.org.uk
  This site aims to help Christians be better equipped to communicate and defend their faith when coming into contact with those of other religions and world views. Christian articles examining: occultism, wicca, witchcraft, paganism, spiritualism, Mormonism, Jehovah's Witnesses, the New Age movement. Also articles on ethics, issues, apologetics and theology.
- Reachout Trust: www.reachouttrust.org
  Reachout Trust is an international evangelical Christian ministry dedicated to equipping the Christian church, upholding evangelical biblical truth, and building bridges to people in the cults, the occult and New Age.
- Ex-Witch Ministries: www.exwitch.org
  A well-balanced site run by former witches, pagans and occultists. The site exists to lead pagans and occultists to Christ and educate the Christian church in issues relating

to occultism. Also has a very useful and active online community forum.

- Refuge Ministries: www.refugeministries.cc
Website of former Satanist now Christian, Jeff Harshbarger. Those who run this site offer much in the way of practical help and have a real Christ-like heart in helping the hurting.
- Free Minds: www.freeminds.org
Watchers of the Watchtower World. Website of Randall Watters, a former Jehovah's Witness who served in various prominent positions in the Watchtower, including the organization's main headquarters. As well as being a good resource for information on Jehovah's Witnesses, this site also contains good general information on mind control and spiritual abuse issues.
- CARM (The Christian Apologetics and Research Ministry) www.carm.org
A large, well established and well maintained evangelical site which exists to equip Christians and refute error.

From Witchcraft to Christ

by Doreen Irvine

From poverty, drugs and prostitution to a life of joy and freedom, this true story charts one woman's entanglement with the occult and her eventual dramatic release.

A classic Christian testimony, Doreen's story is as relevant today as when it was first published. Her experiences may be extreme, yet it still offers hope . . . especially to those who consider purity to be a lost ideal, or who believe they are too far gone to be forgiven.

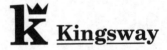 **Kingsway**